Table of Contents

Part 1: Introduction to SQL for Data Analysis

1. What is SQL, and why is it Important?
2. Setting Up Your SQL Environment
3. Installing MySQL/PostgreSQL
4. Importing Datasets
5. Understanding Databases and Tables
6. Relational vs. Non-Relational Databases
7. Schema and Data Types

Part 2: 101 SQL Interview Questions

1. Beginner Level (1-30)
2. Intermediate Level (31-70)
3. Advanced Level (71-101)

Part 3: Solutions to All Questions

102.   Solutions to Beginner Level Questions
103.   Solutions to Intermediate Level Questions
104.   Solutions to Advanced Level Questions

Part 1: Introduction to SQL for Data Analysis

1.1 What is SQL and why is it Important?

SQL, or Structured Query Language, is the standard language used to interact with relational databases. It helps store, retrieve, and manipulate data efficiently. SQL is a fundamental tool for a data analyst because it enables them to extract meaningful insights from large datasets, which is at the core of their job.

Think of SQL as the bridge between raw data and decision-making. Companies collect tons of data—sales records, customer interactions, website traffic, and more—but that data is often scattered across different database tables. SQL allows you to query this data, filter it, join multiple tables, and structure it in a way that helps businesses make informed decisions.

For example, let's say an e-commerce company wants to analyze customer behavior. A data analyst would use SQL to:
- Retrieve all purchase records from the past six months.
- Join data from different tables (e.g., customer info + product details + transactions).
- Identify trends, such as the most popular products or peak shopping hours.

Why is SQL important for a data analyst?

1. Data Extraction & Transformation – Most real-world data is stored in databases. SQL helps analysts pull the right data quickly.
2. Efficiency & Scalability – Unlike Excel, which struggles with large datasets, SQL can handle millions of records efficiently.
3. Automation – Analysts can write queries that automate repetitive tasks, saving time on reporting.
4. Data Integrity – SQL ensures accuracy and consistency when working with structured data. Industry Standard – Whether it's finance, healthcare, or tech, SQL is a must-have skill for working with databases.

1.2 Setting Up Your SQL Environment
- **Installing MySQL/PostgreSQL**
- **Importing Datasets**

Setting Up Your SQL Environment: Installing MySQL/PostgreSQL & Importing Datasets

As a data analyst, setting up an SQL environment is the first step before diving into analysis. The process involves choosing the right database system, installing it, and importing datasets to start querying.

Choosing the Right SQL Database: MySQL vs. PostgreSQL

Both MySQL and PostgreSQL are popular relational database management systems (RDBMS), but they have different strengths:

- MySQL is widely used in web applications and is known for speed and simplicity. It powers platforms like WordPress and e-commerce stores.
- PostgreSQL is more advanced, supporting complex queries, large datasets, and analytical functions, making it great for data analytics and machine learning tasks.

As a data analyst, you might work with either, depending on the company's infrastructure.

1.3 Understanding Databases and Tables
- **Relational vs. Non-Relational Databases**
- **Schema and Data Types**

Relational databases like MySQL and PostgreSQL organize data in structured tables and enforce relationships through primary and foreign keys. They're ideal for structured data and use SQL for querying. On the other hand, NoSQL databases like MongoDB offer flexibility for unstructured or rapidly changing data, storing information in key-value pairs or documents.

When working with databases, understanding schema design is essential, as it defines how data is structured. In relational databases, schema changes require careful planning, whereas NoSQL databases allow for dynamic schema updates. Additionally, choosing the right data types ensures efficiency in storage and query performance. For instance, using **VARCHAR** instead of **TEXT** for short strings saves space and speeds up retrieval times.

■Relational vs. Non-Relational Databases

Databases primarily fall into two broad categories: **relational** and **non-relational**. Let me break them down in simple terms:

1. **Relational Databases (RDBMS)**
   - These databases organize data into structured tables with rows and columns, much like Excel spreadsheets.
   - They follow a strict schema, meaning the structure of the data is predefined (e.g., a table for customers must always have fields like Customer_ID, Name, Email, etc.).
   - Data is connected through **relationships**—for example, a sales table might reference a customer table using a unique Customer_ID.
   - They use **SQL (Structured Query Language)** to query and manipulate data.
   - **Examples**: MySQL, PostgreSQL, SQL Server, Oracle

2. **Use case:** If you're working with structured, transactional data—like sales records, HR databases, or financial reports—relational databases are ideal.

3. **Non-Relational Databases (NoSQL)**
   - Unlike relational databases, these do not use structured tables. Instead, they store data in flexible formats like key-value pairs, documents, graphs, or wide-column stores.
   - They don't require a strict schema, making them more adaptable to unstructured or semi-structured data.
   - These databases are optimized for scalability and speed, especially for handling large datasets with frequent changes.
   - **Examples**: MongoDB (document-based), Redis (key-value store), Cassandra (wide-column store), Neo4j (graph database).

4. **Use case:** If you're dealing with large-scale, evolving datasets—like social media feeds, sensor data from IoT devices, or recommendation engines—NoSQL databases offer more flexibility.

■Schema and Data Types

Now, let's talk about **schemas** and **data types**, which play a key role in data structuring:

1. **Schema**
   - A **schema** is essentially the blueprint of a database—it defines how data is structured, including tables, columns, data types, and relationships.
   - In relational databases, schemas are rigid. If you need to add a new column, you must alter the schema.
   - In NoSQL databases, schemas are flexible, meaning you can add new fields dynamically without predefined structures.

■Installing MySQL/PostgreSQL

Setting up these databases is straightforward:

1. Download the installer from the official MySQL (mysql.com) or PostgreSQL (postgresql.org) website.
2. Run the installation – this typically includes setting up a username, password, and choosing default settings.
3. Set up a graphical interface – Tools like MySQL Workbench or pgAdmin make it easier to interact with databases without using the command line.
4. Start the database server – Once installed, the database must be running for you to connect and execute queries.

■Importing Datasets into SQL

Once the database is set up, the next step is importing data for analysis. Data is usually stored in formats like CSV, Excel, or JSON, and can be imported in multiple ways:

- Using SQL Queries:
  - If the data is already structured, you can create a table and use the `INSERT INTO` statement to add records.

  - Example:

```
CREATE TABLE sales_data (
    id SERIAL PRIMARY KEY,
    customer_name VARCHAR(100),
    product VARCHAR(100),
    purchase_date DATE,
    amount DECIMAL(10,2)
);


INSERT INTO sales_data (customer_name, product, purchase_date, amount)
VALUES ('John Doe', 'Laptop', '2024-04-01', 1200.50);
```

- Using the Import Feature in MySQL Workbench or pgAdmin:
  - Most GUI tools allow you to import CSV or Excel files by mapping columns to a table.
  - Simply navigate to the import/export menu, select the file, and upload it.

- **Using the COPY Command (PostgreSQL-specific):**
  - For large datasets, PostgreSQL has a fast-loading COPY command:

```
COPY sales_data FROM '/path/to/data.csv' DELIMITER ',' CSV HEADER;
```

■Why This Matters for a Data Analyst

Setting up SQL and importing data is a fundamental part of the job because:

✔ Most real-world data lives in databases, and analysts must retrieve and clean it.
✔ Companies deal with large datasets that need structured storage for efficiency.
✔ SQL databases help in performing advanced queries, joins, and aggregations for deeper insights.

Once your environment is ready, you can start writing queries, analyzing trends, and turning raw data into valuable business insights!

Part 2: 101 SQL Questions (Without Solutions)

Questions are categorized into Beginner, Intermediate, and Advanced levels.

Beginner (1-30)

2.1 Retrieve all movies released after 2015 with a rating above 8.0.

Let's assume we have a dataset named movies with the following columns:
- MovieID (Unique identifier)
- Title (Name of the movie)
- ReleaseYear (Year the movie was released)
- Rating (IMDb or any other rating out of 10)
- Genre (Category of the movie)

MovieID	Title	ReleaseYear	Rating	Genre
101	Interstellar	2014	8.6	Sci-Fi
102	Mad Max: Fury Road	2015	8.1	Action
103	La La Land	2016	8.5	Musical
104	Parasite	2019	8.6	Thriller
105	Joker	2019	8.4	Drama
106	The Irishman	2019	7.8	Crime
107	Dune	2021	8.2	Sci-Fi

Expected Output

Title	ReleaseYear	Rating	Genre
La La Land	2016	8.5	Musical
Parasite	2019	8.6	Thriller
Joker	2019	8.4	Drama
Dune	2021	8.2	Sci-Fi

(Solution Page no - 91)

2.2 Find the total number of customers in the database.

Let's assume we have a dataset named customers with the following columns:
- CustomerID (Unique identifier for each customer)
- Name (Customer's name)
- Email (Customer's email)
- SignupDate (Date the customer registered)
- Country (Customer's location)

Sample Data in the customers Table

Example:
- In a relational database (MySQL):

```
CREATE TABLE Customers (
    CustomerID INT PRIMARY KEY,
    Name VARCHAR(255),
    Email VARCHAR(255),
    SignupDate DATE
);
```

- In a NoSQL document database (MongoDB), we might store a customer record as:

json

```
{
    "CustomerID": 101,
    "Name": "John Doe",
    "Email": "johndoe@example.com",
    "SignupDate": "2024-04-04",
    "Preferences": ["Electronics", "Books"]
}
```

Data Types

Every database uses **data types** to ensure that data is stored consistently. Some common data types include:

- Integer (INT) – Whole numbers
- Float/Decimal (FLOAT, DECIMAL) – Numbers with decimals, useful for prices
- String (VARCHAR, TEXT) – Names, descriptions, etc.
- Date & Time (DATE, TIMESTAMP) – Dates and timestamps
- Boolean (BOOLEAN) – True/False values

Choosing the right data type is crucial for optimizing performance. For example, storing a phone number as an **integer** instead of a **string** can lead to issues (like losing leading zeros).

CustomerID	Name	Email	SignupDate	Country
101	Aditi Sharma	aditi@example.com	2023-01-15	India
102	John Smith	john@example.com	2022-11-30	USA
103	Li Wei	liwei@example.com	2023-02-20	China
104	Fatima Khan	fatima@example.com	2023-03-12	UAE
105	Carlos Ruiz	carlos@example.com	2022-12-05	Mexico
106	Priya Patel	priya@example.com	2023-04-18	India

Expected Output

Total_Customers

6

(Solution Page no - 91)

2.3 List all unique product categories in the store.

Let's assume we have a dataset named products with the following columns:
- ProductID (Unique identifier for each product)
- ProductName (Name of the product)
- Category (Product category)
- Price (Price of the product)
- StockQuantity (Available stock)

Sample Data in the products Table

ProductID	ProductName	Category	Price	StockQuantity
201	Denim Jacket	Clothing	1999	20
202	Wireless Earbuds	Electronics	2999	15
203	Running Shoes	Footwear	3499	10
204	Yoga Mat	Fitness	999	25
205	Laptop Stand	Accessories	1299	18
206	Leather Wallet	Accessories	899	30

Expected Output

Category

Clothing

Electronics

Footwear

Fitness

Accessories

(Solution Page no - 92)

2.4 Retrieve all orders placed in the last 30 days.

Let's assume we have a dataset named orders with the following columns:
- OrderID (Unique identifier for each order)
- CustomerID (Reference to the customer who placed the order)
- OrderDate (Date when the order was placed)
- TotalAmount (Total order value)
- Status (Current order status)

Sample Data in the orders Table

OrderID	CustomerID	OrderDate	TotalAmount	Status
501	101	2025-03-05	2500	Shipped
502	102	2025-03-20	1800	Delivered
503	103	2025-03-25	3200	Pending
504	104	2025-04-02	1500	Shipped
505	105	2025-04-03	4200	Delivered
506	106	2025-02-28	2100	Cancelled

Expected Output (Assuming Today's Date is 2025-04-04)

OrderID	CustomerID	OrderDate	TotalAmount	Status
501	101	2025-03-05	2500	Shipped
502	102	2025-03-20	1800	Delivered
503	103	2025-03-25	3200	Pending
504	104	2025-04-02	1500	Shipped
505	105	2025-04-03	4200	Delivered

(Solution Page no - 92)

2.5 Find the total number of orders per customer.

Let's assume we have an orders table with the following columns:
- OrderID (Unique identifier for each order)
- CustomerID (Reference to the customer who placed the order)
- OrderDate (Date when the order was placed)
- TotalAmount (Total order value)
- Status (Current order status)

Sample Data in the orders Table

OrderID	CustomerID	OrderDate	TotalAmount	Status
501	101	2025-03-05	2500	Shipped
502	102	2025-03-20	1800	Delivered
503	103	2025-03-25	3200	Pending
504	101	2025-04-02	1500	Shipped
505	102	2025-04-03	4200	Delivered
506	103	2025-04-04	2100	Delivered

Expected Output

CustomerID	Total_Orders
101	2
102	2
103	2

(Solution Page no - 93)

2.6 Extract customers who have not placed any orders.

To find customers who have never placed an order, we need two tables:
1. customers **Table** (Contains all registered customers)
2. orders **Table** (Contains all customer orders)

Sample Data in the customers Table

CustomerID	Name	Email	SignupDate	Country
101	Aditi Sharma	aditi@example.com	2023-01-15	India
102	John Smith	john@example.com	2022-11-30	USA
103	Li Wei	liwei@example.com	2023-02-20	China
104	Fatima Khan	fatima@example.com	2023-03-12	UAE

| 105 | Carlos Ruiz | carlos@example.com | 2022-12-05 | Mexico |
| 106 | Priya Patel | priya@example.com | 2023-04-18 | India |

Sample Data in the orders Table

OrderID	CustomerID	OrderDate	TotalAmount	Status
501	101	2025-03-05	2500	Shipped
502	102	2025-03-20	1800	Delivered
503	103	2025-03-25	3200	Pending
504	101	2025-04-02	1500	Shipped
505	102	2025-04-03	4200	Delivered
506	103	2025-04-04	2100	Delivered

Expected Output (Customers Without Orders)

CustomerID	Name	Email	SignupDate	Country
104	Fatima Khan	fatima@example.com	2023-03-12	UAE
105	Carlos Ruiz	carlos@example.com	2022-12-05	Mexico
106	Priya Patel	priya@example.com	2023-04-18	India

(Solution Page no - 93)

2.7 Get the top 10 highest-priced products.

To find the top 10 most expensive products in a store, we need a products table that contains pricing details.

Sample Data in the products Table

ProductID	ProductName	Category	Price	StockQuantity
201	Gaming Laptop	Electronics	85000	10
202	Smart TV 55"	Electronics	60000	8
203	Leather Sofa	Furniture	75000	5
204	DSLR Camera	Electronics	55000	12
205	iPhone 15 Pro	Mobile	140000	15
206	Running Shoes	Footwear	8000	20

Expected Output (Top 10 Most Expensive Products)

ProductID	ProductName	Category	Price	StockQuantity

205	iPhone 15 Pro	Mobile	140000	15
201	Gaming Laptop	Electronics	85000	10
203	Leather Sofa	Furniture	75000	5
202	Smart TV 55"	Electronics	60000	8
204	DSLR Camera	Electronics	55000	12

(Solution Page no - 94)

2.8 Count the number of employees in each department.

To determine the number of employees in each department, we need an employees table with department details.

Sample Data in the employees Table

EmployeeID	Name	Department	Position	Salary
101	Aditi Sharma	IT	Software Engineer	70000
102	John Smith	HR	HR Manager	60000
103	Li Wei	IT	Data Analyst	75000
104	Fatima Khan	Finance	Accountant	65000
105	Carlos Ruiz	IT	System Admin	72000
106	Priya Patel	HR	Recruiter	58000

Expected Output (Employees per Department)

Department	Employee_Count
IT	3
HR	2
Finance	1

(Solution Page no - 94)

2.9 Retrieve all products that cost more than the average price.

To find products that are priced above the average, we need a products table containing price details.

Sample Data in the products Table

ProductID	ProductName	Category	Price	StockQuantity
201	Gaming Laptop	Electronics	85000	10
202	Smart TV 55"	Electronics	60000	8
203	Leather Sofa	Furniture	75000	5

204	DSLR Camera	Electronics	55000	12
205	iPhone 15 Pro	Mobile	140000	15
206	Running Shoes	Footwear	8000	20

Expected Output (Products Above the Average Price)

ProductID	ProductName	Category	Price
205	iPhone 15 Pro	Mobile	140000
201	Gaming Laptop	Electronics	85000
203	Leather Sofa	Furniture	75000

(Solution Page no - 95)

2.10 Find customers who are from the same city.

To find customers residing in the same city, we need a customers table that contains city information.

Sample Data in the customers Table

CustomerID	Name	Email	City	Country
101	Aditi Sharma	aditi@example.com	Delhi	India
102	John Smith	john@example.com	New York	USA
103	Li Wei	liwei@example.com	Beijing	China
104	Fatima Khan	fatima@example.com	Dubai	UAE
105	Carlos Ruiz	carlos@example.com	New York	USA
106	Priya Patel	priya@example.com	Delhi	India

Expected Output (Customers from the Same City)

City	Customers
Delhi	Aditi Sharma, Priya Patel
New York	John Smith, Carlos Ruiz

(Solution Page no - 95)

2.11 Retrieve the total revenue generated by each product category.

To calculate the total revenue generated by each product category, we need two tables:
- products (to get product details, including category and price)
- orders (to get the quantity sold for each product)

Sample Data in the products Table

ProductID	ProductName	Category	Price

201	Gaming Laptop	Electronics	85000
202	Smart TV 55"	Electronics	60000
203	Leather Sofa	Furniture	75000
204	DSLR Camera	Electronics	55000
205	iPhone 15 Pro	Mobile	140000
206	Running Shoes	Footwear	8000

Sample Data in the orders Table

OrderID	ProductID	Quantity
301	201	2
302	202	1
303	203	3
304	204	2
305	205	1
306	206	5

Expected Output (Total Revenue Per Category)

Category	Total_Revenue
Electronics	285000
Furniture	225000
Mobile	140000
Footwear	40000

(Solution Page no - 96)

2.12 Get the first and last order date for each customer.

To determine the **first and last order date** for each customer, we need an orders table that contains customer details along with order dates.

Sample Data in the orders Table

OrderID	CustomerID	OrderDate
101	1	2024-01-10
102	2	2024-02-15
103	1	2024-03-05
104	3	2024-01-25
105	2	2024-04-01

| 106 | 1 | 2024-06-18 |

Expected Output (First & Last Order Date per Customer)

CustomerID	First_Order_Date	Last_Order_Date
1	2024-01-10	2024-06-18
2	2024-02-15	2024-04-01
3	2024-01-25	2024-01-25

(Solution Page no - 96)

2.13 Find the number of orders placed per month.

To determine the total number of orders per month, we need an orders table that includes order dates.

Sample Data in the orders Table

OrderID	CustomerID	OrderDate
101	1	2024-01-10
102	2	2024-01-15
103	3	2024-02-05
104	1	2024-02-20
105	2	2024-03-07
106	3	2024-03-22

Expected Output (Orders Per Month)

Order_Month	Total_Orders
2024-01	2
2024-02	2
2024-03	2

(Solution Page no - 97)

2.14 Retrieve the highest and lowest salaries in each department.

To determine the highest and lowest salaries in each department, we need an employees table that includes department names and salaries.

Sample Data in the employees Table

EmployeeID	Name	Department	Salary
101	Aditi Sharma	IT	90000

102	John Smith	HR	70000
103	Li Wei	IT	120000
104	Fatima Khan	Finance	95000
105	Carlos Ruiz	HR	50000
106	Priya Patel	Finance	88000

Expected Output (Highest & Lowest Salary per Department)

Department	Highest_Salary	Lowest_Salary
IT	120000	90000
HR	70000	50000
Finance	95000	88000

(Solution Page no - 97)

2.15 Retrieve the highest and lowest salaries in each department.

To determine the top 5 most frequently purchased products, we need an orders table that includes product IDs and quantities ordered.

Sample Data in the orders Table

OrderID	ProductID	ProductName	Quantity
101	201	Wireless Headphones	5
102	202	Gaming Laptop	2
103	203	Smart TV 55"	4
104	201	Wireless Headphones	3
105	204	Coffee Maker	6
106	205	Running Shoes	7

Expected Output (Top 5 Most Purchased Products)

ProductID	ProductName	Total_Purchased
205	Running Shoes	7
204	Coffee Maker	6
201	Wireless Headphones	8
203	Smart TV 55"	4
202	Gaming Laptop	2

(Solution Page no - 98)

2.16 Retrieve the highest and lowest salaries in each department.

To find customers who made exactly 2 purchases, we need an orders table with customer IDs and their order records.

Sample Data in the orders Table

OrderID	CustomerID	OrderDate
101	1	2024-01-05
102	2	2024-01-08
103	1	2024-02-10
104	3	2024-03-01
105	2	2024-03-15
106	4	2024-04-10

Expected Output

CustomerID
1
2

(Solution Page no - 98)

2.17 Calculate the total sales per region.

To calculate total sales per region, we need order-level data with a Region column and the TotalAmount (or a Quantity × Price calculation).

Sample Data in the orders Table

OrderID	CustomerID	Region	TotalAmount
101	1	North	1500
102	2	South	2000
103	3	East	1750
104	4	North	1200
105	5	South	1800
106	6	West	1000

Expected Output

Region	Total_Sales
South	3800

North	2700
East	1750
West	1000

(Solution Page no - 99)

2.18 Find employees who joined before 2015.

To answer this, we need an employees table that includes employee names and their joining dates.

Sample Data in the employees Table

EmployeeID	Name	Department	JoinDate
101	Aditi Sharma	IT	2012-06-10
102	John Smith	HR	2014-03-25
103	Priya Patel	Finance	2016-07-19
104	Carlos Ruiz	IT	2018-01-15
105	Fatima Khan	HR	2013-11-05
106	Li Wei	Sales	2015-09-30

Expected Output

EmployeeID	Name	Department	JoinDate
101	Aditi Sharma	IT	2012-06-10
102	John Smith	HR	2014-03-25
105	Fatima Khan	HR	2013-11-05

(Solution Page no - 99)

2.19 Retrieve all transactions made between 9 AM and 5 PM.

To get transactions within standard business hours (9:00 AM to 5:00 PM), we'll work with a table containing transaction timestamps.

■ Sample Data in the transactions Table

TransactionID	CustomerID	Amount	TransactionTime
101	1	₹500	2024-03-12 08:45:00
102	2	₹1200	2024-03-12 09:15:00
103	3	₹750	2024-03-12 11:45:00
104	4	₹2000	2024-03-12 14:05:00

| 105 | 5 | ₹300 | 2024-03-12 17:30:00 |
| 106 | 6 | ₹850 | 2024-03-12 16:50:00 |

Expected Output

TransactionID	CustomerID	Amount	TransactionTime
102	2	₹1200	2024-03-12 09:15:00
103	3	₹750	2024-03-12 11:45:00
104	4	₹2000	2024-03-12 14:05:00
106	6	₹850	2024-03-12 16:50:00

(Solution Page no - 100)

2.20 Find the most common product category in sales.

To identify the most frequently sold product category, we need a dataset that includes sales data with a ProductCategory field.

Sample Data in the sales Table

SaleID	ProductID	ProductCategory	Quantity
101	P001	Electronics	3
102	P002	Clothing	5
103	P003	Electronics	2
104	P004	Home Appliances	1
105	P005	Clothing	4
106	P006	Electronics	6

Goal

We want to find the product category that has the highest total quantity sold — which tells us what customers are buying most.

Expected Output

ProductCategory	TotalSold
Electronics	11

(Solution Page no - 100)

2.21 Retrieve customers who have spent more than $500.

To find customers whose total spending exceeds $500, we need access to transaction or order-level data that includes both the CustomerID and the amount spent.

Sample Data from orders Table

OrderID	CustomerID	TotalAmount
201	C001	250
202	C002	600
203	C001	300
204	C003	150
205	C004	700
206	C002	200

Expected Output

CustomerID	TotalSpent
C001	550
C002	800
C004	700

(Solution Page no - 100)

2.22 Get the average order value for each customer.

To determine how much each customer spends on average per order, we'll use order-level data with CustomerID and TotalAmount for each purchase.

Sample Data in orders Table

OrderID	CustomerID	TotalAmount
101	C001	300
102	C002	450
103	C001	200
104	C003	600
105	C002	150
106	C004	500

Expected Output

CustomerID	AvgOrderValue
C001	250.00
C002	300.00
C003	600.00

C004   500.00

(Solution Page no - 101)

2.23 Find the percentage contribution of each product to total sales.

To understand how much each product contributes to the total revenue, we'll calculate the percentage share of each product's sales compared to all products.

Sample Data from sales Table

SaleID	ProductID	ProductName	SaleAmount
101	P001	Wireless Mouse	200
102	P002	Bluetooth Speaker	500
103	P003	USB Cable	100
104	P001	Wireless Mouse	300
105	P004	Keyboard	400
106	P002	Bluetooth Speaker	300

Expected Output

ProductID	ProductName	TotalProductSales	PercentageContribution
P002	Bluetooth Speaker	800	34.78%
P001	Wireless Mouse	500	21.74%
P004	Keyboard	400	17.39%
P003	USB Cable	100	4.35%

(Solution Page no - 101)

2.24 Retrieve customers who have placed an order but never returned.

This type of query is often used in customer retention and behavioral analysis. Our goal is to identify customers who made purchases but didn't return any items — a valuable segment to study, as they may represent satisfied or low-risk customers.

Sample Data from orders Table

OrderID	CustomerID	ProductID	ReturnStatus
101	C001	P001	Not Returned
102	C002	P002	Returned
103	C003	P003	Not Returned
104	C001	P004	Not Returned
105	C004	P005	Returned

106	C005	P006	Not Returned

Expected Output

CustomerID

C001

C003

C005

(Solution Page no - 102)

2.25 Find the highest-selling product in each month.

This query helps identify which products performed the best month-over-month, which is crucial for inventory planning, marketing strategies, and seasonal analysis.

Sample Data from sales Table

SaleID	ProductID	ProductName	SaleAmount	SaleDate
101	P001	Wireless Mouse	300	2024-01-10
102	P002	Bluetooth Speaker	500	2024-01-15
103	P003	USB Cable	200	2024-02-05
104	P002	Bluetooth Speaker	400	2024-02-20
105	P004	Keyboard	600	2024-03-01
106	P001	Wireless Mouse	350	2024-03-15

Expected Output

Month	ProductID	ProductName	TotalSales
2024-01-01	P002	Bluetooth Speaker	500
2024-02-01	P002	Bluetooth Speaker	400
2024-03-01	P004	Keyboard	600

(Solution Page no - 102)

2.26 Count the number of employees per job role.

This query helps in understanding workforce distribution — like how many people are in technical roles, support roles, management, etc. It's important for resource planning, recruitment forecasting, and organizational structuring.

Sample Data from employees Table

EmployeeID	Name	JobRole	Department
E001	Anjali Rao	Data Analyst	Analytics

E002	Rahul Mehra	Data Scientist	Analytics
E003	Tina Verma	Data Analyst	Analytics
E004	Aarav Gupta	HR Executive	HR
E005	Meena Nair	Software Engineer	IT
E006	Mohan Das	Software Engineer	IT

Expected Output

JobRole	NumberOfEmployees
Data Analyst	2
Software Engineer	2
Data Scientist	1
HR Executive	1

(Solution Page no - 103)

2.27 Retrieve all orders where the discount applied is greater than 20%.

This kind of query is useful when the business wants to track high-discount transactions — possibly to analyze their impact on profit margins, identify over-discounting patterns, or review promotional effectiveness.

Sample Data from orders Table

OrderID	CustomerID	ProductID	OrderAmount	Discount (%)
101	C001	P001	1000	15
102	C002	P003	750	25
103	C004	P005	500	30
104	C003	P002	900	10
105	C001	P004	1100	22
106	C005	P006	800	5

Expected Output

OrderID	CustomerID	ProductID	OrderAmount	Discount (%)
102	C002	P003	750	25
103	C004	P005	500	30
105	C001	P004	1100	22

(Solution Page no - 103)

2.28 Get all orders placed on a weekend.

Understanding when customers place orders—especially if they lean toward weekends—can help optimize marketing campaigns, customer support hours, and stock planning. This query helps uncover behavioral trends by filtering orders that happened on Saturday or Sunday.

Sample Data from orders Table

OrderID	CustomerID	OrderDate	OrderAmount
201	C001	2024-03-01	1200
202	C002	2024-03-02	800
203	C003	2024-03-03	950
204	C004	2024-03-05	1100
205	C005	2024-03-09	600
206	C006	2024-03-11	700

Let's assume:
- 2024-03-02 = Saturday
- 2024-03-03 = Sunday
- 2024-03-09 = Saturday

Expected Output

OrderID	CustomerID	OrderDate	OrderAmount
202	C002	2024-03-02	800
203	C003	2024-03-03	950
205	C005	2024-03-09	600

(Solution Page no - 104)

2.29 Retrieve the most popular payment method.

This analysis is great for understanding customer preferences and streamlining the checkout experience. Knowing the most-used payment method can help in reducing transaction friction, negotiating fees with payment partners, and designing better UX flows.

Sample Data from orders Table

OrderID	CustomerID	PaymentMethod	OrderAmount
301	C001	Credit Card	1200
302	C002	UPI	850
303	C003	Credit Card	950
304	C004	Net Banking	760
305	C005	UPI	1100

| 306 | C006 | Credit Card | 980 |

Expected Output

PaymentMethod	UsageCount
Credit Card	3

(Solution Page no - 104)

2.30 Find the longest-serving employee in each department.

Identifying the longest-serving employees in each department is valuable for HR and management to recognize loyalty, mentor potential, and institutional knowledge. It's also helpful for succession planning and performance evaluations.

Sample Data from employees Table

EmployeeID	Name	Department	JoinDate
E101	Anjali	Marketing	2014-02-15
E102	Raj	Sales	2016-06-20
E103	Meena	Marketing	2018-09-10
E104	John	Sales	2013-01-10
E105	Zoya	IT	2015-04-01
E106	Aman	IT	2012-11-05

Expected Output

Department	Name	JoinDate
Marketing	Anjali	2014-02-15
Sales	John	2013-01-10
IT	Aman	2012-11-05

(Solution Page no - 105)

Intermediate Level (31-70)

2.31 Find the top 5 highest-grossing movies.

Identify the top 5 movies based on total revenue — essentially, those that grossed the highest amount.

Sample Dataset: movies Table

MovieID	Title	ReleaseYear	Revenue (in millions)
M001	The Grand Voyage	2018	850
M002	Skyfall Returns	2019	920
M003	The Hidden Code	2020	670
M004	Infinity Quest	2021	1045
M005	Legacy of Shadows	2017	560
M006	Titan Reign	2022	980

Output:

Title	Revenue (in millions)
Infinity Quest	1045
Titan Reign	980
Skyfall Returns	920
The Grand Voyage	850
The Hidden Code	670

(Solution Page no - 106)

2.32 Calculate the total revenue generated per country.

We want to aggregate total revenue across all transactions grouped by country, which helps understand geographic performance.

Sample Dataset: sales Table

SaleID	Country	Product	Revenue (in USD)
S001	USA	Laptop	1,200
S002	Canada	Headphones	200
S003	USA	Smartphone	900
S004	Germany	Laptop	1,100
S005	Canada	Tablet	400
S006	Germany	Smartphone	950

Output:

Country	TotalRevenue (USD)
USA	2,100
Canada	600
Germany	2,050

(Solution Page no - 106)

2.33 Retrieve the first purchase date for each customer.

We want to identify the **first (earliest) purchase date** for each customer — basically, when each customer made their very first transaction.

Sample Dataset: orders Table

OrderID	CustomerID	PurchaseDate
O001	C001	2023-01-12
O002	C002	2023-02-15
O003	C001	2023-03-20
O004	C003	2023-01-18
O005	C002	2023-01-10
O006	C004	2023-03-05

Output:

CustomerID	FirstPurchaseDate
C001	2023-01-12
C002	2023-01-10
C003	2023-01-18
C004	2023-03-05

(Solution Page no - 107)

2.34 Find customers who have purchased more than 5 different products.

We want to identify customers who have purchased more than 5 unique products — this helps understand customer diversity in product consumption.

Sample Dataset: orders Table

OrderID	CustomerID	ProductID	PurchaseDate
O001	C001	P001	2023-01-12
O002	C001	P002	2023-01-15

O003	C001	P003	2023-01-20
O004	C001	P004	2023-01-25
O005	C001	P005	2023-02-01
O006	C001	P006	2023-02-10
O007	C002	P001	2023-01-12
O008	C002	P002	2023-01-14
O009	C003	P001	2023-02-18
O010	C003	P001	2023-02-20

Output:

CustomerID	UniqueProducts
C001	6

(Solution Page no - 107)

2.35 Retrieve employees who have more than 5 years of experience.

To determine if an employee has **more than 5 years** of experience, we need to **calculate the difference between today's date and their join date**, then filter those who've been with the company longer than 5 years.
Assuming today's date is '2025-04-04'.

Sample Dataset: employees Table

EmployeeID	Name	Department	JoinDate
E001	Priya Sharma	Marketing	2016-02-10
E002	Raj Verma	Sales	2018-07-25
E003	Nisha Patel	HR	2013-11-15
E004	Arjun Mehta	IT	2020-01-01
E005	Meena Gupta	Finance	2017-05-30
E006	Rakesh Yadav	IT	2010-08-19

Output:

EmployeeID	Name	Department	JoinDate	YearsOfExperience
E001	Priya Sharma	Marketing	2016-02-10	9
E003	Nisha Patel	HR	2013-11-15	11
E005	Meena Gupta	Finance	2017-05-30	7

| E006 | Rakesh Yadav | IT | 2010-08-19 | 14 |

(Solution Page no - 107)

2.36 Get all transactions where the total amount is greater than twice the average order value.

Sample Dataset: orders Table

Let's assume this is our basic dataset for the question:

OrderID	CustomerID	OrderDate	TotalAmount
O001	C001	2024-12-01	150
O002	C002	2024-12-02	400
O003	C003	2024-12-03	250
O004	C004	2024-12-04	100
O005	C005	2024-12-05	300
O006	C006	2024-12-06	800

█ Output:

OrderID	CustomerID	OrderDate	TotalAmount
O006	C006	2024-12-06	800

(Solution Page no - 108)

2.37 Retrieve the products that have never been sold.

Sample Dataset

Let's assume we're working with two tables:
products table:

ProductID	ProductName	Category
P001	Leather Wallet	Accessories
P002	Running Shoes	Footwear
P003	Bluetooth Speaker	Electronics
P004	Denim Jacket	Apparel
P005	Yoga Mat	Fitness
P006	Laptop Sleeve	Accessories

order_items table:

OrderItemID	OrderID	ProductID	Quantity
OI001	O001	P001	2
OI002	O002	P002	1
OI003	O003	P004	1
OI004	O004	P001	1
OI005	O005	P003	3

● Note: P005 (Yoga Mat) and P006 (Laptop Sleeve) are not in the order_items table — so they've never been sold.

Output:

ProductID	ProductName	Category
P005	Yoga Mat	Fitness
P006	Laptop Sleeve	Accessories

(Solution Page no - 108)

2.38 Find the month with the highest revenue.

Sample Dataset

Let's assume we're working with the following simplified orders table that contains order data:

OrderID	OrderDate	TotalAmount
O001	2024-01-15	450
O002	2024-01-20	200
O003	2024-02-10	900
O004	2024-02-25	100
O005	2024-03-03	700
O006	2024-02-15	400

Output:
After grouping and summing:

OrderMonth	TotalRevenue
2024-02	1400
2024-03	700
2024-01	650

● *Answer: February 2024 has the highest revenue of 1400.*
(Solution Page no - 109)

2.39 Retrieve customers who have purchased the same product more than once.

Sample Dataset — OrderDetails Table
Let's assume we're working with the following table that includes customer purchases:

OrderID	CustomerID	ProductID	Quantity
O001	C001	P101	1
O002	C002	P102	2
O003	C001	P101	1
O004	C003	P103	1
O005	C001	P102	1
O006	C002	P102	1

Result Table:

CustomerID	ProductID	PurchaseCount
C001	P101	2
C002	P102	2

(Solution Page no - 109)

2.40 Count the number of distinct product categories sold each month.

Sample Datasets
Let's assume we're using two tables:
1. Orders Table:

OrderID	OrderDate
O001	2024-01-15
O002	2024-01-20
O003	2024-02-05
O004	2024-02-18
O005	2024-02-25
O006	2024-03-03

2. OrderDetails Table:

OrderID	ProductID
O001	P101
O002	P102

O003	P103
O004	P101
O005	P104
O006	P105

3. Products **Table**:

ProductID	Category
P101	Electronics
P102	Clothing
P103	Home Decor
P104	Clothing
P105	Electronics

Expected Output:

Month	DistinctCategoriesSold
2024-01	2
2024-02	3
2024-03	1

(Solution Page no - 110)

2.41 Find all customers who have placed orders in more than one country.

This kind of question checks your ability to combine data from multiple sources, apply grouping and filtering logic, and answer a meaningful business query.

Sample Dataset
Let's assume we are working with these simplified tables:

1. Customers **Table**:

CustomerID	Name
C001	Alice
C002	Bob
C003	Charlie
C004	Diana
C005	Ethan

2. Orders **Table:**

OrderID	CustomerID	Country
O101	C001	USA
O102	C001	Canada
O103	C002	USA
O104	C003	USA
O105	C003	USA
O106	C004	UK
O107	C004	UK
O108	C005	Germany
O109	C005	France

Expected Output:

CustomerID	Name
C001	Alice
C005	Ethan

(Solution Page no - 111)

2.42 Calculate the moving average of monthly sales.

This question dives into time-series analysis, and calculating the moving average helps smooth out fluctuations to spot trends more clearly — something super relevant in sales forecasting.

Sample Dataset: Monthly Sales
Let's assume we have the following table for monthly sales:

Month	Sales
Jan 2023	1000
Feb 2023	1200
Mar 2023	900
Apr 2023	1500
May 2023	1700
Jun 2023	1600

Output Table: Moving Average (3-month window)

Month	Sales	3-Month Moving Avg

Jan 2023	1000	-
Feb 2023	1200	-
Mar 2023	900	1033.33
Apr 2023	1500	1200.00
May 2023	1700	1366.67
Jun 2023	1600	1600.00

(Solution Page no - 111)

2.43 Retrieve the top 3 highest revenue-generating regions.

Sample Dataset: Sales Table

Order_ID	Region	Product	Quantity	Price
101	North	Laptop	2	800
102	South	Phone	3	300
103	East	Headphones	5	50
104	West	Laptop	1	800
105	North	Phone	4	300
106	South	Laptop	1	800

Final Output: Top 3 Revenue-Generating Regions

Rank	Region	Total_Revenue
1	North	2800
2	South	1700
3	West	800

(Solution Page no - 112)

2.44 Get the highest-rated products in each category.

Sample Dataset: Products Table

Product_ID	Product_Name	Category	Rating
201	Ultra Laptop	Electronics	4.8
202	Noise Earbuds	Electronics	4.6
203	Organic Shampoo	Beauty	4.2
204	Matte Lipstick	Beauty	4.7
205	Trail Running Shoes	Footwear	4.5

206	Leather Boots	Footwear	4.6

Final Output: Highest-Rated Products per Category

Category	Product_Name	Rating
Electronics	Ultra Laptop	4.8
Beauty	Matte Lipstick	4.7
Footwear	Leather Boots	4.6

(Solution Page no - 113)

2.45 Find employees who have referred more than 3 other employees.

Sample Dataset: Employees Table

Employee_ID	Name	Referred_By
101	Alice	NULL
102	Bob	101
103	Charlie	101
104	David	101
105	Eva	102
106	Frank	101

Output Table: Employees who referred more than 3 others

Referrer_ID	Name	Referral_Count
101	Alice	4

(Solution Page no - 113)

2.46 Retrieve orders that contain multiple products.

Sample Dataset: OrderDetails Table

Order_ID	Product_ID	Quantity	Price
201	P01	1	100
201	P02	2	150
202	P03	1	200
203	P04	1	100
203	P05	1	120
204	P06	1	300

Expected Output: Orders with more than one product

Order_ID	Product_Count
201	2
203	2

(Solution Page no - 114)

2.47 Retrieve orders that contain multiple products.

Sample Dataset: UserLogins Table

User_ID	Login_Date
U001	2024-03-01
U001	2024-03-02
U001	2024-03-03
U001	2024-03-04
U001	2024-03-05
U001	2024-03-06
U002	2024-03-01
U002	2024-03-02
U003	2024-03-05
U003	2024-03-06
U003	2024-03-07
U003	2024-03-08
U003	2024-03-09
U003	2024-03-10
U004	2024-03-01

Intermediate Result: Users with Login Count > 5

User_ID	Month	Login_Count
U001	2024-03	6
U003	2024-03	6

■ Final Answer: 2 users (U001 and U003) logged in more than 5 times in March 2024.
(Solution Page no - 114)

2.48 Find the percentage of repeat customers.

Sample Dataset: Orders Table

Order_ID	Customer_ID	Order_Date
O101	C001	2024-03-01
O102	C002	2024-03-02
O103	C001	2024-03-10
O104	C003	2024-03-05
O105	C004	2024-03-06
O106	C002	2024-03-15

(Solution Page no - 115)

2.49 Retrieve products that are priced in the top 10% of all products.

Sample Dataset: Products Table

Product_ID	Product_Name	Price ($)
P001	Classic T-Shirt	25
P002	Premium Hoodie	60
P003	Designer Jacket	150
P004	Basic Sneakers	40
P005	Luxury Leather Bag	300
P006	Sports Watch	200
P007	Denim Jeans	80
P008	Casual Cap	20
P009	High-end Sunglasses	220
P010	Silk Scarf	100

Final Result – Products in Top 10% Price:

Product_ID	Product_Name	Price ($)
P005	Luxury Leather Bag	300
P009	High-end Sunglasses	220

(Solution Page no - 115)

2.50 Find the city with the most orders placed.

Sample Dataset

Let's assume we are working with an Orders table that looks something like this:

Order_ID	Customer_ID	Order_Date	City
O001	C101	2023-01-10	Mumbai
O002	C102	2023-01-11	Delhi
O003	C103	2023-01-12	Mumbai
O004	C104	2023-01-13	Bangalore
O005	C105	2023-01-14	Mumbai
O006	C106	2023-01-15	Delhi

Aggregated Result:

City	Number_of_Orders
Mumbai	3
Delhi	2
Bangalore	1

■ The city with the most orders placed is: Mumbai (3 orders)
(Solution Page no - 116)

2.51 Retrieve all customers who have ordered more than the average order value.

Sample Dataset
We'll assume a simplified dataset structure with orders from customers and the order amounts:

Order_ID	Customer_ID	Order_Value
O001	C101	200
O002	C102	450
O003	C103	300
O004	C104	150
O005	C105	500
O006	C106	100

Output Table

Customer_ID	Order_Value
C102	450
C103	300
C105	500

(Solution Page no - 116)

■These three customers placed orders above the average order value of 283.33.

2.52 Find products that are frequently purchased together.

Sample Datasets
1. Orders

OrderID	CustomerID	OrderDate
201	C001	2023-06-01
202	C002	2023-06-02
203	C001	2023-06-03
204	C003	2023-06-04
205	C004	2023-06-05

2. OrderDetails

OrderID	ProductID
201	P101
201	P102
202	P101
202	P103
203	P101
203	P102
204	P103
204	P104
205	P101
205	P102

3. Products

ProductID	ProductName
P101	Coffee Beans
P102	French Press
P103	Tea Leaves
P104	Ceramic Mug

Expected Output

ProductA	ProductB	TimesBoughtTogether
P101	P102	3

(Solution Page no - 117)

2.53 Retrieve customers who have the highest lifetime value

Sample Datasets

1. Customers

CustomerID	CustomerName
C001	Alice
C002	Bob
C003	Charlie
C004	Diana

2. Orders

OrderID	CustomerID	OrderDate
301	C001	2023-07-01
302	C002	2023-07-03
303	C001	2023-07-04
304	C003	2023-07-05
305	C001	2023-07-06
306	C004	2023-07-06

3. OrderDetails

OrderID	ProductID	Quantity	UnitPrice
301	P201	2	150
301	P202	1	200
302	P203	1	300
303	P201	1	150
304	P202	2	200
305	P204	1	500
306	P203	1	300

Expected Output

CustomerID	CustomerName	LifetimeValue
C001	Alice	1050

❦ Breakdown of Alice's Lifetime Value:
- Order 301: 2×150 + 1×200 = 500
- Order 303: 1×150 = 150
- Order 305: 1×500 = 500
    Total = 500 + 150 + 500 = 1050

(Solution Page no - 118)

2.54 Find employees who have the highest number of direct reports.

Sample Dataset: Employees

EmployeeID	Name	ManagerID
E001	Alice	NULL
E002	Bob	E001
E003	Charlie	E001
E004	Diana	E002
E005	Ethan	E001
E006	Fiona	E003

- ManagerID refers to the EmployeeID of their manager.
- NULL means top-level manager (no one manages them).

Expected Output

EmployeeID	ManagerName	DirectReports
E001	Alice	3

(Solution Page no - 118)

2.55 Retrieve all transactions where the total amount exceeds the 90th percentile.

Sample Dataset: Transactions

TransactionID	CustomerID	Amount
T001	C001	100
T002	C002	250
T003	C003	180
T004	C004	400
T005	C005	220

T006	C006	600

Expected Output
The 90th percentile in this dataset lies between 400 and 600, so:

TransactionID	CustomerID	Amount
T006	C006	600

(Solution Page no - 119)

2.56 Find the average time between customer orders.

Sample Dataset: Orders

OrderID	CustomerID	OrderDate
101	C001	2023-06-01
102	C002	2023-06-02
103	C001	2023-06-05
104	C001	2023-06-10
105	C002	2023-06-06
106	C003	2023-06-07

Expected Output

CustomerID	AvgDaysBetweenOrders
C001	4
C002	4

(Solution Page no - 120)

2.57 Retrieve orders where the shipping time was longer than expected.

Sample Dataset: Orders

OrderID	CustomerID	OrderDate	ExpectedShipDate	ActualShipDate
201	C001	2023-07-01	2023-07-05	2023-07-06
202	C002	2023-07-02	2023-07-06	2023-07-05
203	C003	2023-07-03	2023-07-07	2023-07-10
204	C004	2023-07-04	2023-07-08	2023-07-08
205	C005	2023-07-05	2023-07-09	2023-07-13
206	C006	2023-07-06	2023-07-10	2023-07-09

Expected Output

OrderID	CustomerID	OrderDate	ExpectedShipDate	ActualShipDate	DelayInDays
201	C001	2023-07-01	2023-07-05	2023-07-06	1
203	C003	2023-07-03	2023-07-07	2023-07-10	3
205	C005	2023-07-05	2023-07-09	2023-07-13	4

(Solution Page no - 121)

2.58 Count the number of unique visitors to an e-commerce site.

Sample Dataset: WebsiteVisits

VisitID	UserID	VisitDate	PageViewed
V001	U001	2023-08-01	Home
V002	U002	2023-08-01	Product Page
V003	U001	2023-08-02	Checkout
V004	U003	2023-08-02	Home
V005	U002	2023-08-03	Cart
V006	U004	2023-08-03	Product Page

Expected Output

UniqueVisitors
4

(Solution Page no - 121)

2.59 Retrieve the most purchased brand in each product category.

Sample Dataset: Sales

SaleID	ProductCategory	Brand	Quantity
1	Electronics	Samsung	5
2	Electronics	Apple	8
3	Electronics	Samsung	3
4	Clothing	Nike	6
5	Clothing	Adidas	9
6	Clothing	Nike	4

Expected Output

ProductCategory	Brand	TotalQuantity
Electronics	Apple	8
Clothing	Adidas	9

(Solution Page no - 122)

2.60 Find the revenue contribution of each sales representative.

Sample Dataset: Sales

SaleID	SalesRep	Customer	Revenue
101	Alice	C001	500
102	Bob	C002	700
103	Alice	C003	300
104	Carol	C004	900
105	Bob	C005	400
106	Alice	C006	800

Expected Output

SalesRep	TotalRevenue	RevenueContributionPercent
Alice	1600	44.44%
Bob	1100	30.56%
Carol	900	25.00%

(Solution Page no - 123)

2.61 Retrieve employees who have worked in more than one department.

Sample Dataset: EmployeeDepartmentHistory

EmployeeID	EmployeeName	Department	StartDate
E001	Alice	HR	2022-01-01
E002	Bob	Finance	2022-02-01
E001	Alice	IT	2023-03-01
E003	Carol	Finance	2021-07-01
E004	Dave	HR	2022-08-15
E002	Bob	Marketing	2023-04-01

Expected Output

EmployeeID	EmployeeName	DepartmentCount
E001	Alice	2
E002	Bob	2

(Solution Page no - 123)

2.62 Find customers who have placed orders on their birthdays.

Sample Datasets
1. Customers

CustomerID	CustomerName	DOB
C001	Alice	1990-06-15
C002	Bob	1985-12-01
C003	Carol	1992-04-10
C004	Dave	1991-06-15

2. Orders

OrderID	CustomerID	OrderDate	Amount
O101	C001	2023-06-15	250
O102	C002	2023-11-30	300
O103	C003	2023-04-10	150
O104	C004	2023-06-16	200
O105	C001	2023-07-01	100

Expected Output

CustomerID	CustomerName	DOB	OrderID	OrderDate	Amount
C001	Alice	1990-06-15	O101	2023-06-15	250
C003	Carol	1992-04-10	O103	2023-04-10	150

(Solution Page no - 124)

2.63 Retrieve all orders where the payment method changed after checkout.

Sample Datasets
1. Orders

OrderID	CustomerID	CheckoutPaymentMethod
O1001	C001	Credit Card

O1002	C002	UPI
O1003	C003	PayPal
O1004	C004	UPI
O1005	C005	Credit Card

2. Payments

OrderID	FinalPaymentMethod	PaymentDate
O1001	Credit Card	2023-06-10
O1002	Credit Card	2023-06-11
O1003	PayPal	2023-06-11
O1004	Net Banking	2023-06-12
O1005	Credit Card	2023-06-12

Expected Output

OrderID	CustomerID	CheckoutPaymentMethod	FinalPaymentMethod	PaymentDate
O1002	C002	UPI	Credit Card	2023-06-11
O1004	C004	UPI	Net Banking	2023-06-12

(Solution Page no - 125)

2.64 Find products that had the highest sales increase month over month.

Sample Dataset: Sales

ProductID	ProductName	SaleMonth	TotalSales
P001	Sneakers	2024-01	1000
P001	Sneakers	2024-02	1800
P002	Hoodie	2024-01	500
P002	Hoodie	2024-02	700
P003	T-shirt	2024-01	800
P003	T-shirt	2024-02	750

Expected Output

ProductID	ProductName	SaleMonth	TotalSales	PrevMonthSales	SalesGrowth
P001	Sneakers	2024-02	1800	1000	800

(Solution Page no - 126)

2.65 Retrieve the number of orders that were canceled before shipment.

Sample Datasets

1. Orders

OrderID	CustomerID	OrderDate	OrderStatus	CancelDate
O1001	C001	2024-01-05	Cancelled	2024-01-06
O1002	C002	2024-01-06	Shipped	NULL
O1003	C003	2024-01-07	Cancelled	2024-01-08
O1004	C004	2024-01-08	Shipped	NULL
O1005	C005	2024-01-09	Cancelled	2024-01-10

2. Shipments

OrderID	ShipmentDate
O1002	2024-01-07
O1004	2024-01-09
O1005	2024-01-11

Expected Output

CancelledBeforeShipment

2

(Solution Page no - 126)

2.66 Count the number of customers who have made a second purchase.

Sample Dataset: Orders

OrderID	CustomerID	OrderDate
O1001	C001	2024-01-01
O1002	C002	2024-01-02
O1003	C001	2024-01-05
O1004	C003	2024-01-10
O1005	C002	2024-01-12
O1006	C001	2024-01-20

Expected Output

CustomersWithSecondPurchase

2

Because **CustomerID C001** has 3 orders and **C002** has 2 — both have made a second purchase.
(Solution Page no - 127)

2.67 Find employees who have received the highest bonuses.

Sample Datasets
1. Employees

EmployeeID	Name	Department
E001	Alice	Sales
E002	Bob	Marketing
E003	Charlie	HR
E004	Diana	Sales
E005	Edward	IT

2. Bonuses

EmployeeID	BonusAmount	BonusYear
E001	8000	2024
E002	5000	2024
E003	9000	2024
E004	9000	2024
E005	4000	2024

Expected Output

EmployeeID	Name	Department	BonusAmount
E003	Charlie	HR	9000
E004	Diana	Sales	9000

Both Charlie and Diana received the highest bonus of 9000.
(Solution Page no - 127)

2.68 Retrieve all transactions made during promotional periods.

Sample Datasets
1. Transactions

TransactionID	CustomerID	TransactionDate	Amount
T001	C001	2024-12-01	500
T002	C002	2024-12-05	1200
T003	C003	2024-12-15	700

T004	C004	2024-12-20	300
T005	C005	2024-12-30	950

2. Promotions

PromoID	PromoName	StartDate	EndDate
P01	Winter Bonanza	2024-12-01	2024-12-10
P02	Holiday Special	2024-12-25	2024-12-31

Expected Output

TransactionID	CustomerID	TransactionDate	Amount	PromoName
T001	C001	2024-12-01	500	Winter Bonanza
T002	C002	2024-12-05	1200	Winter Bonanza
T005	C005	2024-12-30	950	Holiday Special

(Solution Page no - 128)

2.69 Find the most common customer complaint category.

Sample Dataset: CustomerComplaints

ComplaintID	CustomerID	ComplaintCategory	ComplaintDate
CMP001	C001	Late Delivery	2024-12-01
CMP002	C002	Damaged Product	2024-12-02
CMP003	C003	Late Delivery	2024-12-03
CMP004	C004	Wrong Item	2024-12-04
CMP005	C005	Late Delivery	2024-12-05
CMP006	C006	Damaged Product	2024-12-06

Expected Output

ComplaintCategory	ComplaintCount
Late Delivery	3

(Solution Page no - 129)

2.70 Retrieve employees who have completed the most training programs.

Sample Datasets
1. Employees

EmployeeID	Name	Department
E001	Alice	Sales

E002	Bob	HR
E003	Charlie	IT
E004	Diana	Marketing
E005	Edward	Sales

2. EmployeeTraining

TrainingID	EmployeeID	TrainingName	CompletionDate
T001	E001	Communication Skills	2024-06-01
T002	E002	Diversity & Inclusion	2024-06-05
T003	E001	Advanced Sales	2024-06-10
T004	E003	Data Security Basics	2024-06-12
T005	E001	Time Management	2024-06-20
T006	E004	Creative Marketing	2024-06-22

Expected Output

EmployeeID	Name	Department	TrainingCompleted
E001	Alice	Sales	3

(Solution Page no - 129)

Advanced (71-101) Level

2.71 Rank products by sales volume using window functions.

Rank products by sales volume using window functions" is a classic SQL question — ideal for showcasing your understanding of aggregations, window functions, and product performance metrics.

Sample Datasets
1. Products

ProductID	ProductName	Category
P001	Wireless Mouse	Electronics
P002	Bluetooth Speaker	Electronics
P003	Yoga Mat	Fitness
P004	Coffee Maker	Home
P005	Water Bottle	Fitness

2. Sales

SaleID	ProductID	Quantity	SaleDate
S001	P001	10	2024-11-01
S002	P002	15	2024-11-02
S003	P003	8	2024-11-03
S004	P001	5	2024-11-04
S005	P005	20	2024-11-05
S006	P002	10	2024-11-06

Expected Output

ProductID	ProductName	TotalQuantity	SalesRank
P002	Bluetooth Speaker	25	1
P005	Water Bottle	20	2
P001	Wireless Mouse	15	3
P003	Yoga Mat	8	4

(Solution Page no - 130)

2.72 Find customers who made multiple purchases in the same month.

Find customers who made multiple purchases in the same month" is a strong test of your ability to manipulate dates, group data, and use HAVING clauses — all common in real-world analytics.

Sample Datasets
1. Customers

CustomerID	CustomerName
C001	Alice
C002	Bob
C003	Charlie
C004	Diana

2. Orders

OrderID	CustomerID	OrderDate	Amount
O001	C001	2024-06-02	120
O002	C002	2024-06-10	250
O003	C001	2024-06-15	180
O004	C003	2024-07-01	300
O005	C001	2024-07-20	90
O006	C002	2024-06-22	200

Expected Output

CustomerID	CustomerName	OrderMonth	OrdersInMonth
C001	Alice	2024-06-01	2
C002	Bob	2024-06-01	2

(Solution Page no - 131)

2.73 Calculate the moving average of daily sales.

Sample Dataset: Sales

SaleID	SaleDate	Amount
S001	2024-06-01	100
S002	2024-06-02	150
S003	2024-06-03	120
S004	2024-06-04	180
S005	2024-06-05	200
S006	2024-06-06	170

Expected Output

SaleDate	DailySales	MovingAvg_3Day
2024-06-01	100	100.00
2024-06-02	150	125.00
2024-06-03	120	123.33
2024-06-04	180	150.00
2024-06-05	200	166.67
2024-06-06	170	183.33

(Solution Page no - 132)

2.74 Retrieve the top 3 customers with the highest lifetime value.

Retrieving the top 3 customers with the highest lifetime value" is a common business ask in customer analytics — it highlights your ability to aggregate sales, rank results, and identify VIPs that drive revenue.

Sample Datasets
1. Customers

CustomerID	CustomerName
C001	Alice
C002	Bob
C003	Charlie
C004	Diana
C005	Ethan

2. Orders

OrderID	CustomerID	OrderDate	Amount
O001	C001	2024-06-01	120
O002	C002	2024-06-02	300
O003	C001	2024-06-10	180
O004	C003	2024-06-11	250
O005	C004	2024-06-13	450
O006	C005	2024-06-15	150
O007	C002	2024-06-18	400

Expected Output

CustomerID	CustomerName	LifetimeValue
C002	Bob	700
C004	Diana	450
C001	Alice	300

(Solution Page no - 132)

2.75 Find the most frequent customer journey path on an e-commerce site.

Find the most frequent customer journey path on an e-commerce site" is a real-world scenario that shows your skill in analyzing behavior patterns and funnel optimization. It highlights how customers typically navigate through an e-commerce platform before converting (or dropping off).

Sample Dataset: Customer_Journey

CustomerID	EventTime	PageName
C001	2024-06-01 10:00:00	Homepage
C001	2024-06-01 10:01:00	ProductPage
C001	2024-06-01 10:03:00	Cart
C001	2024-06-01 10:05:00	Checkout
C002	2024-06-01 10:00:00	Homepage
C002	2024-06-01 10:01:30	ProductPage
C002	2024-06-01 10:04:00	Cart
C003	2024-06-01 11:00:00	Homepage
C003	2024-06-01 11:02:00	ProductPage
C003	2024-06-01 11:03:30	Cart
C003	2024-06-01 11:06:00	Checkout

Each row logs a customer event in timestamp order.

Expected Output

journey_path	frequency
Homepage > ProductPage > Cart	3

(Solution Page no - 133)

2.76 Identify anomalies in transaction data.

Identify anomalies in transaction data" is a classic real-world data analysis task — useful for fraud detection, quality assurance, and system monitoring. In a SQL interview, this question tests how well you spot outliers using statistical or business logic.

Sample Dataset: Transactions

TransactionID	CustomerID	Amount	TransactionDate
T001	C001	100	2024-06-01
T002	C002	120	2024-06-02
T003	C003	105	2024-06-03
T004	C004	980	2024-06-04
T005	C001	110	2024-06-05
T006	C002	115	2024-06-06

You can already spot that **T004** looks suspicious — an outlier in amount.

Expected Output

TransactionID	CustomerID	Amount	TransactionDate
T004	C004	980	2024-06-04

(Solution Page no - 134)

2.77 Retrieve all customers who have downgraded their subscription.

Highlights your ability to analyze behavioral trends, customer churn risk, and lifecycle transitions. Let's dive in and structure this like you're walking an interviewer through the process.

Sample Dataset: Subscription_History

CustomerID	SubscriptionLevel	ChangeDate
C001	Premium	2024-06-01
C001	Basic	2024-09-01
C002	Basic	2024-06-01
C002	Standard	2024-08-01
C003	Standard	2024-05-15
C003	Basic	2024-07-01

This dataset tracks historical changes to each customer's subscription level. A downgrade means moving from a higher to a lower tier.

Let's define subscription levels:
- Premium > Standard > Basic
  For simplicity, we'll rank them numerically.

Expected Output

CustomerID	PreviousLevel	CurrentLevel	ChangeDate
C001	Premium	Basic	2024-09-01
C003	Standard	Basic	2024-07-01

(Solution Page no - 135)

2.78 Find the impact of discounts on total revenue.

Sample Dataset: Orders

OrderID	CustomerID	ProductID	Quantity	UnitPrice	Discount	OrderDate
O001	C001	P001	2	500	0.10	2024-06-01
O002	C002	P002	1	1000	0.00	2024-06-01
O003	C003	P003	3	300	0.20	2024-06-02
O004	C001	P001	1	500	0.00	2024-06-03
O005	C004	P004	2	700	0.15	2024-06-04
O006	C002	P002	1	1000	0.05	2024-06-05

Let's calculate two revenues:
- 🍬 Gross Revenue = Quantity × UnitPrice (before discount)
- 🎯 Net Revenue = Quantity × UnitPrice × (1 - Discount) (after discount)

Expected Output

Gross_Revenue	Net_Revenue	Discount_Impact	Discount_Impact_Percentage
6600	5720	880	13.33%

(Solution Page no - 135)

2.79 Retrieve users who have the longest average session time.

We want to identify users who are highly engaged, measured by how long they typically stay during each session. These users might be your power users or the most valuable ones.

Sample Dataset: UserSessions

SessionID	UserID	SessionStart	SessionEnd
S001	U001	2024-06-01 09:00:00	2024-06-01 09:30:00
S002	U002	2024-06-01 10:00:00	2024-06-01 11:00:00
S003	U001	2024-06-01 11:00:00	2024-06-01 11:20:00
S004	U003	2024-06-01 12:00:00	2024-06-01 12:50:00
S005	U002	2024-06-01 14:00:00	2024-06-01 15:10:00

S006	U004	2024-06-01 15:00:00	2024-06-01 15:30:00

Expected Output

UserID	Avg_Session_Minutes
U002	65.00
U003	50.00
U004	30.00
U001	25.00

(Solution Page no - 136)

2.80 Find the most common reason for order returns.

Q-Identify the most common return reason per product category and calculate its return rate. Additionally, flag categories where return rates exceed 10%

Sample Datasets:
1. Orders

OrderID	CustomerID	ProductID	OrderDate
O101	C001	P001	2024-06-01
O102	C002	P002	2024-06-02
O103	C003	P001	2024-06-03
O104	C004	P003	2024-06-04
O105	C005	P004	2024-06-05
O106	C006	P003	2024-06-06

2. Returns

ReturnID	OrderID	ReturnReason	ReturnDate
R001	O101	Damaged item	2024-06-05
R002	O102	Size too small	2024-06-06
R003	O103	Damaged item	2024-06-07
R004	O106	Color not as shown	2024-06-08

3. Products

ProductID	ProductName	Category
P001	T-Shirt A	Apparel
P002	Sneakers B	Footwear

P003	Jacket C	Apparel
P004	Headphones D	Electronics

Expected Output

Category	Most_Common_Return_Reason	ReturnCount	TotalOrderCount	TotalReturnCount	ReturnRatePercent	ReturnRiskFlag
Apparel	Damaged item	2	4	3	75.00	High Return Rate
Footwear	Size too small	1	1	1	100.00	High Return Rate
Electronics	(null)	(null)	1	0	0.00	Normal

(Solution Page no - 136)

2.81 Retrieve employees with the highest retention rate in each department.

Q-Retrieve employees with the highest retention rate in each department. Include tenure in years, rank within the department, and flag employees who've been with the company more than 5 years."

What This Tests in an Interview
This question checks if the candidate can:
- Join tables
- Use date functions for tenure calculation
- Use window functions (like RANK(), PARTITION BY)
- Apply case logic to flag key attributes (e.g., tenure > 5 years)
- Think business-first by identifying high-retention employees within a department (often useful in HR dashboards, attrition prediction, etc.)

Sample Datasets
Employees

EmpID	Name	DepartmentID	HireDate	ExitDate
E101	Alice	D1	2015-01-10	NULL
E102	Bob	D1	2019-03-15	NULL
E103	Charlie	D2	2016-05-12	2021-05-01
E104	Diana	D2	2013-09-20	NULL
E105	Ethan	D3	2018-06-10	NULL
E106	Fiona	D3	2020-02-01	NULL

Departments

DepartmentID	DepartmentName

D1	Sales
D2	Engineering
D3	HR

Expected Output

EmpID	Name	DepartmentName	HireDate	EndDate	TenureYears	DeptRank	LongTenureFlag
E101	Alice	Sales	2015-01-10	2025-04-07	10.24	1	Yes
E104	Diana	Engineering	2013-09-20	2025-04-07	11.55	1	Yes
E105	Ethan	HR	2018-06-10	2025-04-07	6.82	1	Yes

(Solution Page no - 136)

2.82 Find sales reps who exceeded their targets by the highest percentage.

Q-Which sales representatives exceeded their monthly sales targets by the highest percentage? Provide the total sales, target, percentage exceeded, and rank them accordingly. Also flag those who exceeded by more than 50%

Sample Datasets (5–6 Rows Each)
1. Sales Table

SaleID	SalesRepID	SaleDate	Amount
S001	R1	2024-01-15	15000
S002	R2	2024-01-17	22000
S003	R1	2024-01-20	13000
S004	R3	2024-01-25	9000
S005	R2	2024-01-30	10000
S006	R3	2024-02-02	11000

2. SalesReps Table

SalesRepID	RepName
R1	Alice
R2	Bob
R3	Carol

3. SalesTargets **Table**

SalesRepID	Month	MonthlyTarget
R1	2024-01	20000
R2	2024-01	25000
R3	2024-01	15000

Expected Output Table

SalesRepID	RepName	SaleMonth	TotalSales	MonthlyTarget	PercentOverTarget	ExceededBy50Percent	PerformanceRank
R1	Alice	2024-01	28000	20000	40.00	No	1
R2	Bob	2024-01	32000	25000	28.00	No	2
R3	Carol	2024-01	9000	15000	-40.00	No	3

(Solution Page no - 139)

2.83 Identify trends in customer churn.

Q-Identify monthly trends in customer churn, highlighting churn rate over time, and detect which months had the highest churn. Also, segment churn by subscription plan type.

What This Tests in an Interview
- Temporal data analysis
- Cohort tracking and retention/churn logic
- Advanced SQL constructs: CASE, COUNT(DISTINCT), GROUP BY, window functions
- Business communication: interpreting churn drivers

Sample Datasets (5–6 Rows Each)
Customers

CustomerID	Name	JoinDate	PlanType
C001	Alice	2023-01-05	Premium
C002	Bob	2023-01-15	Basic
C003	Carol	2023-02-10	Premium
C004	David	2023-02-25	Basic
C005	Ella	2023-03-01	Basic
C006	Frank	2023-03-05	Premium

SubscriptionStatus

CustomerID	StatusDate	Status

C001	2023-05-01	Active
C002	2023-04-01	Churned
C003	2023-06-01	Churned
C004	2023-05-01	Active
C005	2023-04-01	Churned
C006	2023-06-01	Active

Expected Output Table

StatusMonth	PlanType	ChurnedCustomers	TotalCustomers	ChurnRate (%)
2023-04-01	Basic	2	3	66.67
2023-04-01	Premium	0	1	0.00
2023-06-01	Premium	1	2	50.00

(Solution Page no - 140)

2.84 Retrieve transactions where the order amount deviates significantly from the average.

Q-Retrieve all transactions where the order amount deviates significantly (more than 2 standard deviations) from the average transaction amount.

What This Tests in an Interview:
- Ability to apply statistical logic in SQL
- Use of window functions, CTEs, and standard deviation
- Understanding of anomaly detection using distribution metrics
- Clear business communication of insights

Sample Datasets (5–6 Rows)
Transactions Table

TransactionID	CustomerID	OrderDate	OrderAmount
T001	C001	2023-06-01	150
T002	C002	2023-06-02	170
T003	C003	2023-06-02	160
T004	C004	2023-06-03	155
T005	C005	2023-06-04	500
T006	C006	2023-06-04	140

📍 In this dataset, T005 (OrderAmount = 500) looks like a potential anomaly.

Expected Output Table

TransactionID	CustomerID	OrderDate	OrderAmount	avg_order	std_order	deviation

T005	C005	2023-06-04	500	212.5	128.46	287.5

(Solution Page no - 141)

2.85 Find the most common time of day for purchases.

Q-Find the most common time of day (Morning, Afternoon, Evening, Night) when purchases are made based on transaction timestamps.

What This Tests in an Interview:
- Use of CASE statements for time categorization
- Understanding of timestamp functions and grouping
- Ability to translate raw datetime values into business-friendly insights
- Comfort with aggregation and ranking

● Sample Dataset: Transactions Table

TransactionID	CustomerID	OrderDateTime	OrderAmount
T001	C001	2024-01-10 08:15:00	250
T002	C002	2024-01-10 13:45:00	300
T003	C003	2024-01-10 19:30:00	200
T004	C004	2024-01-10 22:10:00	150
T005	C005	2024-01-11 07:50:00	275
T006	C006	2024-01-11 14:20:00	325

Expected Output

TimeOfDay	PurchaseCount	Rank
Morning	2	1
Afternoon	2	1

❢ In this case, *Morning* and *Afternoon* are tied as the most common purchase times.
(Solution Page no - 142)

2.86 Retrieve the percentage of customers who upgraded their plans.

Q-Retrieve the percentage of customers who upgraded their plans from a lower tier to a higher tier.

What This Tests in an Interview:
- Use of self-joins or window functions to track changes over time
- Knowledge of ranking events chronologically per user
- Ability to categorize and compare tiers
- Calculating percentages using aggregates and subqueries

● Sample Dataset: CustomerPlans Table

CustomerID	PlanName	PlanTier	ChangeDate

C001	Basic	1	2023-01-01
C001	Premium	3	2023-06-01
C002	Basic	1	2023-03-15
C002	Standard	2	2023-08-01
C003	Premium	3	2023-02-10
C004	Standard	2	2023-01-10

Assumption: Higher number = higher plan tier
e.g., Tier 1 = Basic, Tier 2 = Standard, Tier 3 = Premium

Expected Output

PercentageUpgraded

66.67

Interpretation: 66.67% of customers who made at least two plan changes upgraded.
(Solution Page no - 143)

2.87 Find the correlation between product ratings and return rates.

What Interviewers Are Testing:
- Ability to join and aggregate across multiple tables
- Comfort with calculating ratios and averages
- Knowledge of statistical analysis in SQL, specifically correlation
- Skill in data interpretation

■ Sample Datasets (Tables):
ProductReviews

ProductID	Rating	ReviewDate
P001	4.5	2023-01-10
P002	3.0	2023-02-11
P003	5.0	2023-03-09
P004	2.0	2023-04-01
P005	4.0	2023-05-22

OrderDetails

OrderID	ProductID	IsReturned
O101	P001	0
O102	P002	1
O103	P003	0

O104	P004	1
O105	P005	0
O106	P004	1

Expected Output:

RatingReturnCorrelation

-0.87

Interpretation: There is a strong negative correlation (-0.87), meaning higher product ratings are associated with lower return rates.
(Solution Page no - 144)

2.88 Retrieve employees who have been promoted more than once.

Identify employees who have moved up through the organizational hierarchy multiple times, by analyzing promotion history from role/title changes.

Sample Datasets (5–6 rows each):
EmployeePromotions

EmployeeID	PromotionDate	PreviousTitle	NewTitle
E101	2020-01-15	Junior Analyst	Analyst
E102	2019-02-20	Sales Rep	Senior Sales Rep
E101	2021-04-10	Analyst	Senior Analyst
E103	2020-06-12	Intern	Junior Developer
E101	2022-07-01	Senior Analyst	Lead Analyst
E104	2023-01-10	Developer	Senior Developer

Expected Output:

EmployeeID	PromotionCount
E101	3

(Solution Page no - 144)

2.89 Find regions where the average order value is higher than the global average.

Q-Identify regions where the average order value has consistently exceeded the global monthly average for at least 3 consecutive months.

Sample Dataset:
Orders

OrderID	CustomerID	Region	OrderAmount	OrderDate
O101	C001	North	1200	2023-01-15

O102	C002	North	1300	2023-02-15
O103	C003	North	1250	2023-03-20
O104	C004	South	900	2023-01-25
O105	C005	South	950	2023-02-22
O106	C006	South	850	2023-03-11

Expected Output:

Region	consecutive_months
North	3

(Solution Page no - 145)

2.90 Retrieve customers who have interacted with customer service more than 5 times.

Q-Retrieve customers who have interacted with customer service more than 5 times in the last 6 months, categorized by type of interaction (e.g., complaint, inquiry, technical issue).

Sample Dataset:
CustomerServiceLogs

InteractionID	CustomerID	InteractionType	InteractionDate
INT001	C001	Complaint	2023-11-10
INT002	C001	Inquiry	2023-12-05
INT003	C001	Complaint	2023-12-20
INT004	C001	Technical Issue	2024-01-15
INT005	C001	Complaint	2024-02-05
INT006	C001	Complaint	2024-03-02
INT007	C002	Inquiry	2024-01-08
INT008	C003	Complaint	2024-02-14
INT009	C003	Complaint	2024-03-20
INT010	C003	Complaint	2024-03-28

Expected Output:

CustomerID	InteractionType	InteractionCount	TotalInteractions
C001	Complaint	4	6
C001	Inquiry	1	6
C001	Technical Issue	1	6

(Solution Page no - 146)

2.91 Identify the impact of marketing campaigns on sales volume.

Q-Identify the impact of marketing campaigns on sales volume by comparing average daily sales before, during, and after each campaign.

Sample Datasets (5–6 rows each):
Campaigns

CampaignID	CampaignName	StartDate	EndDate
CMP001	Winter Boost	2024-11-01	2024-11-15
CMP002	New Year Hype	2025-01-01	2025-01-10

Sales

SaleID	SaleDate	Amount	CampaignID
S001	2024-10-25	150	NULL
S002	2024-11-03	200	CMP001
S003	2024-11-05	250	CMP001
S004	2024-11-18	160	NULL
S005	2024-12-31	180	NULL
S006	2025-01-04	400	CMP002

Expected Output Table:

CampaignID	CampaignName	SalePeriod	TotalSales	TotalRevenue	AvgDailySale
CMP001	Winter Boost	Pre-Campaign	1	150.00	150.00
CMP001	Winter Boost	During-Campaign	2	450.00	225.00
CMP001	Winter Boost	Post-Campaign	1	160.00	160.00
CMP002	New Year Hype	Pre-Campaign	1	180.00	180.00
CMP002	New Year Hype	During-Campaign	1	400.00	400.00

(Solution Page no - 147)

2.92 Retrieve the top 10% of customers by spending.

Sample Datasets (5–6 rows each):
Customers

CustomerID	CustomerName
C001	Alice
C002	Bob

C003	Charlie
C004	Diana
C005	Evan
C006	Fatima

Orders

OrderID	CustomerID	OrderAmount	OrderDate
O101	C001	200	2024-11-01
O102	C002	150	2024-11-03
O103	C001	300	2024-11-05
O104	C003	700	2024-11-07
O105	C004	100	2024-11-09
O106	C006	600	2024-11-10
O107	C002	350	2024-11-11
O108	C005	120	2024-11-12

Expected Output Table:

CustomerID	CustomerName	TotalSpent
C003	Charlie	700
C006	Fatima	600

(Solution Page no - 148)

2.93 Find trends in seasonal product sales.

Q-Using the sales and product datasets below, identify trends in seasonal product sales over the last 2 years. Specifically, determine which product categories have peak sales during specific quarters and if any seasonal patterns emerge. Use SQL to support your analysis.

Provided Datasets (sample format)
1. sales

sale_id	product_id	customer_id	sale_date	quantity	total_amount
1	101	1001	2023-01-15	2	40.00
2	102	1002	2023-04-22	1	15.00
3	103	1003	2023-07-05	3	90.00
4	104	1004	2023-11-18	2	60.00

| 5 | 101 | 1005 | 2024-01-10 | 1 | 20.00 |
| 6 | 102 | 1006 | 2024-04-12 | 2 | 30.00 |

2. products

product_id	product_name	category	price
101	Wool Scarf	Winter Wear	20.00
102	Sunscreen	Summer Care	15.00
103	T-shirt	Summer Wear	30.00
104	Jacket	Winter Wear	30.00

3. customers

customer_id	name	city
1001	Alice	Delhi
1002	Bob	Mumbai
1003	Charlie	Bangalore
1004	David	Jaipur
1005	Eva	Pune
1006	Frank	Kolkata

Expected Output Table:

year	quarter	category	total_units_sold	total_revenue
2023	Q1	Winter Wear	2	40.00
2023	Q2	Summer Care	1	15.00
2023	Q3	Summer Wear	3	90.00
2023	Q4	Winter Wear	2	60.00
2024	Q1	Winter Wear	1	20.00
2024	Q2	Summer Care	2	30.00

(Solution Page no - 149)

2.94 Identify customers who have abandoned carts frequently.

Q-Using the provided datasets, identify customers who frequently add items to the cart but do not complete the purchase. List the top repeat offenders with the number of abandoned carts over the past 6 months.

Sample Datasets

1. customers

customer_id	name	email
1001	Alice	alice@gmail.com
1002	Bob	bob@yahoo.com
1003	Charlie	charlie@gmail.com
1004	David	david@gmail.com

2. products

product_id	product_name	category	price
201	Hoodie	Winter Wear	40.00
202	Sunglasses	Summer Wear	25.00
203	Jeans	Casual Wear	35.00

3. cart

cart_id	customer_id	product_id	added_date	purchased_flag
1	1001	201	2023-10-10	FALSE
2	1002	203	2023-11-20	TRUE
3	1003	202	2023-11-25	FALSE
4	1001	203	2023-12-05	FALSE
5	1004	201	2024-01-10	FALSE
6	1001	202	2024-02-10	FALSE
7	1003	201	2024-03-15	FALSE

4. orders

order_id	customer_id	product_id	order_date
1	1002	203	2023-11-20

5. sessions

session_id	customer_id	session_date	device
501	1001	2024-02-10	Mobile
502	1003	2024-03-15	Desktop

Expected Output:

customer_id	name	email	abandoned_cart_count
1001	Alice	alice@gmail.com	3

1003   Charlie charlie@gmail.com 2
(Solution Page no - 150)

2.95 Retrieve orders where the actual delivery time was significantly delayed.

Q-Using the provided datasets, retrieve orders where the actual delivery time was significantly delayed (i.e., more than 3 days over the expected delivery date). List the affected customers, order details, and delay duration.

Provided Datasets (5 tables)
1. customers

customer_id	name	email	city
1	Alice	alice@gmail.com	Delhi
2	Bob	bob@yahoo.com	Mumbai
3	Charlie	charlie@outlook.com	Pune
4	Diana	diana@gmail.com	Chennai

2. products

product_id	product_name	category	price
101	Hoodie	Winter Wear	40.00
102	Sunglasses	Summer Wear	25.00
103	Jeans	Casual Wear	35.00

3. orders

order_id	customer_id	product_id	order_date	expected_delivery_date
201	1	101	2024-12-01	2024-12-05
202	2	102	2024-12-03	2024-12-07
203	3	103	2024-12-05	2024-12-10
204	1	102	2024-12-10	2024-12-14

4. deliveries

delivery_id	order_id	actual_delivery_date
501	201	2024-12-06
502	202	2024-12-12
503	203	2024-12-17
504	204	2024-12-18

5. shipping_partners

partner_id	name	rating
1	Delhivery	4.1
2	Blue Dart	3.8
3	Ecom Express	4.3

Expected Output Table:

order_id	customer_name	product_name	order_date	expected_delivery_date	actual_delivery_date	delay_days
203	Charlie	Jeans	2024-12-05	2024-12-10	2024-12-17	7
202	Bob	Sunglasses	2024-12-03	2024-12-07	2024-12-12	5

(Solution Page no - 150)

2.96 Find the impact of social media engagement on customer purchases.

Q-Using the provided datasets, analyze how social media engagement influences customer purchases. Identify patterns such as whether highly engaged users convert more, and which platforms drive the most revenue

Provided Datasets (6 Tables)
1. customers

customer_id	name	email	signup_date
1	Alice	alice@gmail.com	2023-01-10
2	Bob	bob@yahoo.com	2023-03-05
3	Charlie	charlie@gmail.com	2023-05-15
4	Diana	diana@gmail.com	2023-07-22

2. social_media_engagement

engagement_id	customer_id	platform	likes	comments	shares	engagement_date
101	1	Instagram	5	2	1	2023-12-01
102	2	Facebook	10	3	0	2023-12-05
103	3	Instagram	1	0	0	2023-12-10
104	1	Instagram	7	3	2	2024-01-15
105	2	Facebook	3	1	0	2024-01-20
106	4	Twitter	12	6	3	2024-01-25

3. products

product_id	product_name	category	price
201	Hoodie	Winter Wear	40.00
202	Sunglasses	Summer Wear	25.00
203	Jeans	Casual Wear	35.00

4. orders

order_id	customer_id	product_id	order_date	total_amount
301	1	201	2024-01-20	40.00
302	2	203	2024-01-22	35.00
303	4	202	2024-02-01	25.00

5. sessions

session_id	customer_id	session_date	device	source
601	1	2024-01-19	Mobile	Instagram
602	2	2024-01-20	Desktop	Facebook
603	3	2024-01-20	Mobile	Instagram
604	4	2024-01-30	Mobile	Twitter

6. platform_metrics

platform	avg_engagement_score
Instagram	4.5
Facebook	3.8
Twitter	5.2

Expected Output Table:

customer_id	name	platform	total_engagement_score	order_count	total_spent
4	Diana	Twitter	36	1	25.00
1	Alice	Instagram	25	1	40.00
2	Bob	Facebook	20	1	35.00
3	Charlie	Instagram	1	0	NULL

(Solution Page no - 151)

2.97 Retrieve all orders where the shipping address was modified post-purchase.

Retrieve all orders where the shipping address was modified after the order was placed. Include customer name, old and new addresses, and how many days after the purchase the change occurred.

Provided Datasets (6 Tables)
1. customers

customer_id	name	email
1	Alice	alice@gmail.com
2	Bob	bob@yahoo.com
3	Charlie	charlie@outlook.com
4	Diana	diana@gmail.com

2. orders

order_id	customer_id	product_id	order_date	shipping_address_id
101	1	301	2024-01-10	1001
102	2	302	2024-01-15	1002
103	3	303	2024-01-20	1003
104	1	304	2024-01-25	1004

3. shipping_address_changes

change_id	order_id	old_address	new_address	change_date
201	101	A-10, Delhi	B-20, Delhi	2024-01-12
202	104	5 Park Lane, Noida	9 Lake Rd, Gurgaon	2024-01-29

4. products

product_id	product_name	category	price
301	Hoodie	Winter Wear	40.00
302	Jeans	Casual Wear	35.00
303	Cap	Summer Wear	15.00
304	Sneakers	Footwear	50.00

5. shipping_partners

partner_id	name	rating
1	Blue Dart	4.2
2	Delhivery	3.9

3	Ecom Express	4.1

6. order_shipping

order_id	partner_id	tracking_id	delivery_status
101	1	BLU123	Shipped
102	2	DEL456	Delivered
103	3	ECOM789	Pending
104	1	BLU999	In Transit

Expected Output Table:

order_id	customer_name	product_name	order_date	old_address	new_address	change_date	days_after_order
104	Alice	Sneakers	2024-01-25	5 Park Lane, Noida	9 Lake Rd, Gurgaon	2024-01-29	4
101	Alice	Hoodie	2024-01-10	A-10, Delhi	B-20, Delhi	2024-01-12	2

(Solution Page no - 152)

2.98 Identify fraudulent transaction patterns.

Q-Identify potentially fraudulent transactions based on patterns such as high-value orders placed shortly after account creation, multiple failed transactions before a success, or multiple orders from different cities within a short time window.

Provided Datasets (6 Tables)
1. customers

customer_id	name	email	signup_date
1	Alice	alice@gmail.com	2024-01-01
2	Bob	bob@yahoo.com	2024-02-20
3	Charlie	charlie@outlook.com	2024-03-10

2. transactions

txn_id	customer_id	amount	status	txn_date	city
101	1	200.00	Success	2024-01-05	Delhi
102	1	220.00	Success	2024-01-06	Delhi
103	2	900.00	Failed	2024-02-21	Mumbai
104	2	850.00	Failed	2024-02-21	Mumbai

105	2		880.00	Success	2024-02-21	Mumbai
106	3		1000.00	Success	2024-03-11	Chennai
107	3		1050.00	Success	2024-03-11	Kolkata

3. orders

order_id	txn_id	product_id	order_status	delivery_address
201	101	301	Delivered	Delhi
202	102	302	Delivered	Delhi
203	105	303	Processing	Mumbai
204	106	304	Delivered	Chennai
205	107	305	Processing	Kolkata

4. products

product_id	product_name	category	price
301	Laptop Bag	Accessories	200.00
302	Earbuds	Electronics	220.00
303	Smartwatch	Electronics	880.00
304	Phone	Electronics	1000.00
305	Phone	Electronics	1050.00

5. failed_txn_logs

log_id	customer_id	txn_id	reason	log_time
1	2	103	Card declined	2024-02-21
2	2	104	Invalid OTP	2024-02-21

6. devices

customer_id	device_id	location	login_time
1	D1	Delhi	2024-01-05
2	D2	Mumbai	2024-02-21
3	D3	Chennai	2024-03-11
3	D4	Kolkata	2024-03-11

Expected Output Table:

customer_id	name	txn_id	amount	txn_date	reason
2	Bob	105	880.00	2024-02-21	Multiple failed txns before success
3	Charlie	106	1000.00	2024-03-11	High amount shortly after signup
3	Charlie	107	1050.00	2024-03-11	Multiple city orders same day

(Solution Page no - 153)

2.99 Find the correlation between product reviews and sales performance.

Q-Find the correlation between average product review ratings and their total sales quantity. Highlight the top-performing products by both metrics and assess whether higher-rated products also sell more

Provided Datasets (6 Tables)
1. products

product_id	product_name	category	price
101	Denim Jacket	Clothing	50.00
102	Bluetooth Earbuds	Electronics	70.00
103	Yoga Mat	Fitness	20.00
104	LED Lamp	Home Decor	30.00
105	Wireless Mouse	Electronics	25.00

2. product_reviews

review_id	product_id	customer_id	rating	review_date
1	101	1	4	2024-01-10
2	101	2	5	2024-01-12
3	102	3	3	2024-01-15
4	102	1	2	2024-01-18
5	103	2	4	2024-01-20
6	104	3	5	2024-01-22
7	105	1	3	2024-01-25

3. orders

order_id	customer_id	order_date	total_amount
301	1	2024-01-10	120.00
302	2	2024-01-12	150.00

| 303 | 3 | 2024-01-14 | 45.00 |
| 304 | 1 | 2024-01-18 | 75.00 |

4. order_items

order_id	product_id	quantity	price
301	101	1	50.00
301	103	1	20.00
301	105	2	25.00
302	102	2	70.00
303	104	1	30.00
304	102	1	70.00

5. customers

customer_id	name	email
1	Alice	alice@gmail.com
2	Bob	bob@yahoo.com
3	Charlie	charlie@outlook.com

6. categories

category_id	category_name
1	Clothing
2	Electronics
3	Fitness
4	Home Decor

Expected Output Table:

product_id	product_name	category	avg_rating	total_reviews	total_units_sold	total_revenue
104	LED Lamp	Home Decor	5.00	1	1	30.00
101	Denim Jacket	Clothing	4.50	2	1	50.00
103	Yoga Mat	Fitness	4.00	1	1	20.00
105	Wireless Mouse	Electronics	3.00	1	2	50.00

| 102 | Bluetooth Earbuds | Electronics | 2.50 | 2 | 3 | 210.00 |

(Solution Page no - 154)

2.100 Retrieve the average number of items per order per month.

Q-Retrieve the average number of items per order per month. Make sure to consider multiple items in a single order and display monthly trends.

Assumed Datasets (5 Tables)

1. orders

order_id	customer_id	order_date
301	1	2024-01-10
302	2	2024-01-12
303	3	2024-02-05
304	1	2024-02-18
305	2	2024-03-01

2. order_items

order_id	product_id	quantity	price
301	101	2	50.00
301	105	1	25.00
302	102	1	70.00
303	104	2	30.00
304	102	3	70.00
305	103	1	20.00
305	104	1	30.00

3. products

product_id	product_name	category
101	Denim Jacket	Clothing
102	Bluetooth Earbuds	Electronics
103	Yoga Mat	Fitness
104	LED Lamp	Home Decor
105	Wireless Mouse	Electronics

4. customers

customer_id	name	email
1	Alice	alice@gmail.com
2	Bob	bob@yahoo.com
3	Charlie	charlie@outlook.com

5. categories

category_id	category_name
1	Clothing
2	Electronics
3	Fitness
4	Home Decor

Expected Output Table:

order_month	total_orders	total_items_in_month	avg_items_per_order
1	2	4	2.00
2	2	5	2.50
3	1	2	2.00

(Solution Page no - 155)

2.101 Identify the most profitable customer segment.

Identify the most profitable customer segment based on total revenue generated. Segment customers by location, age group, or gender (or a combination) and rank the segments by their total purchase amount.

Assumed Datasets (6 Tables)
1. customers

customer_id	name	email	age	gender	city
1	Alice	alice@gmail.com	27	F	Mumbai
2	Bob	bob@yahoo.com	34	M	Delhi
3	Charlie	charlie@outlook.com	22	M	Bangalore
4	Nidhi	nidhi@gmail.com	45	F	Mumbai

2. orders

order_id	customer_id	order_date	total_amount
301	1	2024-01-10	120.00

302	2	2024-01-12	150.00
303	3	2024-02-05	45.00
304	1	2024-02-18	75.00
305	4	2024-03-01	180.00

3. order_items

order_id	product_id	quantity	price
301	101	1	50.00
301	103	1	20.00
301	105	2	25.00
302	102	2	70.00
303	104	1	30.00
304	102	1	70.00
305	101	2	50.00
305	104	1	30.00

4. products

product_id	product_name	category
101	Denim Jacket	Clothing
102	Bluetooth Earbuds	Electronics
103	Yoga Mat	Fitness
104	LED Lamp	Home Decor
105	Wireless Mouse	Electronics

5. categories

category_id	category_name
1	Clothing
2	Electronics
3	Fitness
4	Home Decor

6. segments (we'll derive dynamically using age groups)

Expected Output Table:

gender	city	age_group	total_revenue
F	Mumbai	45+	180.00
F	Mumbai	25-34	195.00
M	Delhi	35-44	150.00
M	Bangalore	18-24	45.00

(Solution Page no - 156)

Part 3: Solutions to All Questions

Solutions to Beginner Level Questions

2.1 SQL Query to Retrieve Movies Released After 2015 with a Rating Above 8.0

```
SELECT Title, ReleaseYear, Rating, Genre
FROM movies
WHERE ReleaseYear > 2015 AND Rating > 8.0;
```

■How to Explain This in an Interview
If an interviewer asks you to retrieve movies released after 2015 with a rating above 8.0, here's how you can explain your thought process clearly and concisely:
*"To extract the required data, I first identified the relevant columns: ReleaseYear and Rating. Since we need movies released after 2015, we use the condition ReleaseYear > 2015. Additionally, to filter out only high-rated movies, we apply Rating > 8.0.

The SQL query I wrote uses the SELECT statement to fetch only the necessary columns (Title, ReleaseYear, Rating, Genre). The WHERE clause ensures that we only retrieve movies meeting the criteria.

Looking at the dataset, movies like *La La Land*, *Parasite*, *Joker*, and *Dune* fit the condition. The query effectively filters the data while keeping the dataset manageable for analysis. If needed, we could enhance this further by sorting the results using ORDER BY Rating DESC to see the highest-rated movies at the top."*

This explanation demonstrates not just SQL knowledge but also critical thinking about filtering and structuring data effectively.

2.2 SQL Query to Find the Total Number of Customers

To count the total number of customers, we use the COUNT(*) function:

```
SELECT COUNT(*) AS Total_Customers
FROM customers;
```

■How to Explain This in an Interview
If an interviewer asks how you would find the total number of customers, here's how you can respond:

*"To determine the total number of customers in the database, I use the COUNT(*) function, which counts all rows in the customers table. This method ensures that every customer record is included, regardless of the specific columns being considered.

In this case, the dataset has six customer records, so the output of my query is 6. If we needed to count distinct customers based on a specific criterion, like unique email addresses, we could use COUNT(DISTINCT Email).

This approach is useful in business scenarios, such as calculating active users, total registrations, or customer segmentation. Additionally, if I needed more insights, I could group the data by country or signup year using GROUP BY."*

2.3 SQL Query to Retrieve Unique Product Categories.

To list all unique product categories, we use the DISTINCT keyword:

```
SELECT DISTINCT Category
FROM products;
```

■How to Explain This in an Interview

If asked how to find unique product categories in a store's database, you can explain it like this:

*"To identify all unique product categories available in the store, I use the DISTINCT keyword in SQL. This ensures that duplicate category values are eliminated, giving a clean list of all product types.

For example, in our dataset, we have six products belonging to different categories like **Clothing, Electronics, Footwear, Fitness, and Accessories**. Even though 'Accessories' appears twice, DISTINCT ensures it is listed only once.

This type of query is useful in retail and e-commerce analytics, where businesses might want to analyze sales performance by category, track inventory levels, or optimize product listings. If needed, we could enhance this further by **counting** products per category using GROUP BY."*

2.4 SQL Query to Retrieve Orders from the Last 30 Days.

To find orders placed in the last 30 days, we compare OrderDate with the current date using the DATEADD() function in SQL (for SQL Server) or INTERVAL in MySQL/PostgreSQL.

```
SELECT OrderID, CustomerID, OrderDate, TotalAmount, Status
FROM orders
WHERE OrderDate >= CURRENT_DATE - INTERVAL 30 DAY;
```

For SQL Server:

```
SELECT OrderID, CustomerID, OrderDate, TotalAmount, Status
FROM orders
WHERE OrderDate >= DATEADD(DAY, -30, GETDATE());
```

*Note: Order 506 is **not included** since it was placed on 2025-02-28, which is more than 30 days ago.*

■How to Explain This in an Interview
If asked how to find orders placed in the last 30 days, you can explain your thought process like this:
*"To retrieve all orders from the last 30 days, I use a date filter in the WHERE clause. The condition OrderDate >= CURRENT_DATE - INTERVAL 30 DAY ensures we only select orders placed within the last month.

For example, if today's date is April 4, 2025, this query will return orders from March 5, 2025, onwards. In our dataset, orders placed on March 5, March 20, March 25, April 2, and April 3 meet the criteria, while older orders are excluded.
This type of query is useful for tracking recent sales, analyzing customer behavior, and generating business reports. If needed, we could enhance it by filtering only *delivered* orders or grouping results by customer to see repeat buyers."*

2.5 SQL Query to Find Total Orders Per Customer

To count the total number of orders each customer has placed, we use the GROUP BY clause:

```
SELECT CustomerID, COUNT(OrderID) AS Total_Orders
FROM orders
GROUP BY CustomerID;
```

How to Explain This in an Interview

If asked how to find the total number of orders per customer, you can explain your approach like this:
*"To determine how many orders each customer has placed, I use the COUNT() function on OrderID and group the results by CustomerID. The GROUP BY clause ensures that the count is calculated separately for each customer.

For example, in our dataset, **Customers 101, 102, and 103** have each placed **two orders**. This type of analysis is useful for identifying repeat customers, tracking purchase frequency, and segmenting customers based on their buying behavior.
If we wanted more insights, we could join this with a customers table to retrieve customer names or filter by a specific period to see recent activity."*

2.6 SQL Query to Find Customers Without Orders

To extract customers who have not placed any orders, we use a LEFT JOIN with NULL filtering:

```
SELECT c.CustomerID, c.Name, c.Email, c.SignupDate, c.Country
FROM customers c
LEFT JOIN orders o ON c.CustomerID = o.CustomerID
WHERE o.CustomerID IS NULL;
```

How to Explain This in an Interview

If asked how to find customers who have not placed any orders, you can explain your approach like this:
*"To identify customers who have never placed an order, I used a LEFT JOIN between the customers and orders tables. This ensures we retrieve all customers, regardless of whether they have orders.

Then, I filtered the results using WHERE o.CustomerID IS NULL, which ensures we only get customers who don't have matching records in the orders table.

For example, in our dataset, Fatima Khan, Carlos Ruiz, and Priya Patel have not placed any orders. This insight is valuable for business strategies like customer re-engagement, targeted marketing, and retention campaigns.
If needed, we could further analyze why these customers haven't purchased by checking factors like their signup date, location, or email activity."*

2.7 SQL Query to Get the Top 10 Highest-Priced Products

To retrieve the highest-priced products, we use the ORDER BY clause in descending order and limit the results to 10:

```
SELECT ProductID, ProductName, Category, Price, StockQuantity
FROM products
ORDER BY Price DESC
LIMIT 10;
```

For SQL Server:

```
SELECT TOP 10 ProductID, ProductName, Category, Price, StockQuantity
FROM products
ORDER BY Price DESC;
```

■How to Explain This in an Interview

If asked how to find the most expensive products in a store, you can explain your approach like this:
*"To retrieve the highest-priced products, I used the ORDER BY clause on the Price column in descending order, ensuring that the most expensive items appear first. The LIMIT 10 ensures we only fetch the top 10 products.

For example, in our dataset, the iPhone 15 Pro (₹140,000), Gaming Laptop (₹85,000), and Leather Sofa (₹75,000) are among the most expensive products in the store.
This kind of query is useful for businesses looking to track high-value products, optimize pricing strategies, or run targeted marketing campaigns for premium customers. If needed, I could further enhance this query by adding filters based on stock availability or category."*

2.8 SQL Query to Count Employees in Each Department

To count the number of employees in each department, we use the COUNT() function with GROUP BY:

```
SELECT Department, COUNT(EmployeeID) AS Employee_Count
FROM employees
GROUP BY Department;
```

■How to Explain This in an Interview
If asked how to count employees in each department, you can explain your approach like this:
*"To determine the number of employees in each department, I used the COUNT() function on EmployeeID while grouping the results by Department. This ensures that each department is listed with its total number of employees.

For example, in our dataset, the **IT department has 3 employees, HR has 2, and Finance has 1**.

This type of analysis is useful for workforce planning, identifying departments that need hiring, and ensuring balanced workloads across teams. If required, I could enhance this query by filtering based on salary, location, or job position to get more detailed insights."*

2.9 SQL Query to Find Products Above the Average Price

To extract products that are more expensive than the average price, we first calculate the **average price** using a subquery and then filter the products accordingly:

```
SELECT ProductID, ProductName, Category, Price
FROM products
WHERE Price > (SELECT AVG(Price) FROM products);
```

$Average\ Price = 685000 + 60000 + 75000 + 55000 + 140000 + 8000 = 70333.33$

■How to Explain This in an Interview
If asked how to find products that cost more than the average price, you can explain your approach like

this:

*"To retrieve products priced above the average, I first calculated the **average price** of all products using AVG(Price). Then, I used a **subquery** inside the WHERE clause to filter out only those products whose price is greater than this average.

For example, in our dataset, the **iPhone 15 Pro (₹140,000), Gaming Laptop (₹85,000), and Leather Sofa (₹75,000)** are priced above the average price of ₹70,333.

This query is valuable for identifying premium products, setting pricing strategies, and analyzing market trends. If required, I could refine this further by filtering by category or stock availability for deeper insights."*

2.10 SQL Query to Find Customers from the Same City

To group customers by city and list only those cities that have more than one customer, we use HAVING COUNT(*) > 1:

```
SELECT City, GROUP_CONCAT(Name) AS Customers
FROM customers
GROUP BY City
HAVING COUNT(*) > 1;
```

For SQL Server (alternative without GROUP_CONCAT):

```
SELECT c1.City, c1.Name AS Customer1, c2.Name AS Customer2
FROM customers c1
JOIN customers c2 ON c1.City = c2.City AND c1.CustomerID < c2.CustomerID;
```

■How to Explain This in an Interview

If asked how to find customers from the same city, you can explain your approach like this:

*"To find customers living in the same city, I used GROUP BY City along with HAVING COUNT(*) > 1, ensuring that only cities with multiple customers are included in the result.

For example, in our dataset, Aditi Sharma and Priya Patel are from Delhi, while John Smith and Carlos Ruiz are from New York.

This kind of analysis is useful for targeted marketing, city-based promotions, and regional sales strategies. If needed, I could refine this query to include additional filters, such as customer spending behavior or signup dates, to generate deeper insights."*

2.11 SQL Query to Get Total Revenue Per Category

To calculate the total revenue for each product category, we **join** the products and orders tables and use SUM() to aggregate revenue:

```
SELECT p.Category, SUM(p.Price * o.Quantity) AS Total_Revenue
FROM products p
JOIN orders o ON p.ProductID = o.ProductID
GROUP BY p.Category;
```

■How to Explain This in an Interview

If asked how to calculate total revenue by product category, you can explain your approach like this:

*"To find the total revenue for each product category, I joined the products table with the orders table using ProductID, ensuring that each order's quantity is multiplied by the respective product price. Then, I grouped by Category and used SUM() to calculate the total revenue for each category.

For example, in our dataset:
- Electronics generated ₹2,85,000,
- Furniture generated ₹2,25,000,
- Mobile (iPhone 15 Pro) contributed ₹1,40,000,
- Footwear made ₹40,000 in revenue.

This type of analysis is crucial for **business decision-making**, as it helps identify the most profitable product categories, optimize inventory, and plan marketing strategies accordingly. If needed, I could further refine this query by filtering revenue within a specific time period or by store location."*

2.12 SQL Query to Find First and Last Order Date per Customer

To get the first and last order date for each customer, we use the MIN() and MAX() **functions** with GROUP BY CustomerID:

```
SELECT CustomerID,
       MIN(OrderDate) AS First_Order_Date,
       MAX(OrderDate) AS Last_Order_Date
FROM orders
GROUP BY CustomerID;
```

■How to Explain This in an Interview
If asked how to retrieve the first and last order date for each customer, you can explain your approach like this:

*"To find the first and last order dates for each customer, I used the MIN() function to get the earliest order date and the MAX() function to get the most recent order date. The results were grouped by CustomerID to ensure that we get these values per customer.

For example, in our dataset:
- Customer 1 placed their first order on January 10, 2024, and their last order on June 18, 2024.
- Customer 2 had their first order on February 15, 2024, and last order on April 1, 2024.
- Customer 3 placed only one order on January 25, 2024.

This analysis helps businesses understand customer purchase behavior, track retention, and identify inactive customers who may need re-engagement strategies. If required, I could refine this further by adding filters such as order status or total order value to get more insights."*

2.13 SQL Query to Find Number of Orders Per Month

We extract the **month and year** from OrderDate, group by it, and count the number of orders per month:

```
SELECT DATE_FORMAT(OrderDate, '%Y-%m') AS Order_Month, COUNT(*) AS Total_Orders
FROM orders
GROUP BY Order_Month
ORDER BY Order_Month;
```

For **SQL Server** (using FORMAT() instead of DATE_FORMAT()):

```
SELECT FORMAT(OrderDate, 'yyyy-MM') AS Order_Month, COUNT(*) AS Total_Orders
FROM orders
GROUP BY FORMAT(OrderDate, 'yyyy-MM')
ORDER BY Order_Month;
```

■How to Explain This in an Interview
If asked how to find the total number of orders per month, you can explain your approach like this:

*"To calculate the number of orders placed per month, I extracted the **year and month** from the OrderDate field and grouped by it. Using COUNT(*), I aggregated the total number of orders for each month and sorted them chronologically.

For example, in our dataset:
- January 2024 had 2 orders,
- February 2024 had 2 orders,
- March 2024 also had 2 orders.

This analysis is valuable for tracking seasonal trends, sales performance, and forecasting demand. If required, I could refine this further by analyzing order values, product categories, or customer segments to provide deeper insights into revenue trends and customer behavior."*

2.14 SQL Query to Get the Highest and Lowest Salary per Department

We use **MAX() and MIN() functions** with GROUP BY Department to find the highest and lowest salary in each department:

```
SELECT Department,
       MAX(Salary) AS Highest_Salary,
       MIN(Salary) AS Lowest_Salary
FROM employees
GROUP BY Department;
```

■How to Explain This in an Interview
If asked how to find the **highest and lowest salary per department**, you can explain your approach like this:

*"To determine the highest and lowest salary in each department, I used MAX(Salary) to get the highest salary and MIN(Salary) to get the lowest salary while grouping the results by Department.

For example, in our dataset:
- In the **IT department**, the highest salary is **₹1,20,000**, while the lowest is **₹90,000**.
- In **HR**, the highest salary is **₹70,000**, and the lowest is **₹50,000**.
- In **Finance**, the highest salary is **₹95,000**, and the lowest is **₹88,000**.

This analysis is useful for **salary benchmarking, compensation planning, and identifying salary gaps** within departments. If required, I could refine this query further by including **employee names, experience levels, or job titles** to gain more insights into salary distribution."*

2.15 SQL Query to Find the Top 5 Most Purchased Products

To get the top 5 most frequently purchased products, we **sum the quantity** for each product and rank them in descending order:

```
SELECT ProductID, ProductName, SUM(Quantity) AS Total_Purchased
FROM orders
GROUP BY ProductID, ProductName
ORDER BY Total_Purchased DESC
LIMIT 5;
```

■How to Explain This in an Interview
If asked how to find the **top 5 most frequently purchased products**, you can explain your approach like this:
*"To determine the top-selling products, I used SUM(Quantity) to get the total units sold for each product and then ordered them in descending order. Using LIMIT 5, I extracted only the top 5 products.

For example, in our dataset:
- Running Shoes were purchased 7 times, making them the most popular product.
- The coffee Maker was purchased 6 times.
- Wireless Headphones were purchased 8 times across multiple orders.
- Smart TV 55" and Gaming Laptop also made it to the top 5.

This type of analysis helps businesses identify **bestselling products, optimize inventory, and plan marketing strategies**. If required, I could refine the query further by analyzing purchase trends over different time periods or customer segments."*

2.16 SQL Query to Retrieve Customers with Exactly 2 Purchases

To solve this, we count how many times each customer appears in the orders table and filter for exactly 2:

```
SELECT CustomerID
FROM orders
GROUP BY CustomerID
HAVING COUNT(*) = 2;
```

■How to Explain This in an Interview
To find customers who made exactly two purchases, I grouped the orders by CustomerID and used the COUNT(*) function to count how many orders each customer made. I then used the HAVING clause to filter only those customers whose order count is equal to 2.

*In our example dataset, Customers **1 and 2** have placed two orders each, so they are returned in the results.*

*This kind of insight is useful for understanding customer behavior — for instance, identifying people who are **repeating buyers** but haven't yet become high-frequency purchasers. Marketing or retention campaigns can be targeted to this segment to encourage them to purchase more frequently."*

2.17 SQL Query to Calculate Total Sales per Region

We'll use the SUM() function and group the results by region:

```
SELECT Region, SUM(TotalAmount) AS Total_Sales
FROM orders
GROUP BY Region
ORDER BY Total_Sales DESC;
```

■How to Explain This in an Interview
"To calculate the total sales per region, I used the SUM() aggregation on the TotalAmount column and grouped the data by the Region field. This helps us identify which regions are generating the most revenue.
In the given dataset:
- The South region has the highest sales with ₹3,800.
- The North follows with ₹2,700, then East and West with ₹1,750 and ₹1,000 respectively.

This kind of regional sales breakdown is essential for strategic decision-making — whether it's optimizing logistics, planning region-specific promotions, or understanding customer demand patterns. If I had more granular data like product categories or sales reps by region, I could also drill deeper to find what's driving performance in each area."

2.18 SQL Query to Find Employees Who Joined Before 2015

We use a WHERE clause to filter employees based on their joining date:

```
SELECT EmployeeID, Name, Department, JoinDate
FROM employees
WHERE JoinDate < '2015-01-01';
```

How to Explain This in a Data Analyst Interview
"To find employees who joined before the year 2015, I used a simple WHERE clause on the JoinDate column and compared it to '2015-01-01'. This allows me to filter out employees who joined earlier than that specific date.
In our dataset, we found that three employees—**Aditi Sharma**, **John Smith**, and **Fatima Khan**—joined before 2015. This kind of analysis is helpful when a company wants to:
- Recognize long-tenured employees
- Plan for training or leadership programs
- Understand workforce experience across departments

If needed, this could also be extended to include tenure calculations or combined with performance data for more robust insights."

2.19 SQL Query to Retrieve Transactions Between 9 AM and 5 PM

We'll extract the **time portion** of each TransactionTime and filter using the TIME() function:

```
SELECT TransactionID, CustomerID, Amount, TransactionTime
FROM transactions
WHERE TIME(TransactionTime) BETWEEN '09:00:00' AND '17:00:00';
```

■How to Explain This in a Data Analyst Interview
"To filter transactions that occurred during working hours (9 AM to 5 PM), I extracted the time portion from the TransactionTime using the TIME() function and then applied a BETWEEN condition to filter only those rows.

This approach allows us to analyze customer behavior within standard business hours. For example, based on the sample dataset, four transactions occurred within this window — which could be used to identify peak transaction times.

This type of insight can help businesses plan staffing, optimize marketing sends, or understand customer engagement during office hours. If needed, this query could also be modified to analyze hourly trends or compare workday vs. after-hours behavior."

2.20 SQL Query to Find Most Common Product Category

```
SELECT ProductCategory, SUM(Quantity) AS TotalSold
FROM sales
GROUP BY ProductCategory
ORDER BY TotalSold DESC
LIMIT 1;
```

■ How to Explain This in a Data Analyst Interview

"To find the most common product category in terms of sales, I grouped the sales data by ProductCategory and used the SUM() function to total up the quantity sold in each category. Then, I sorted the results in descending order of quantity and used LIMIT 1 to retrieve the top-selling category.

In this dataset, **Electronics** is the most frequently purchased category, with a total of 11 items sold. This kind of analysis helps stakeholders understand what products are driving sales and where to focus marketing or inventory efforts.

If we had more detailed data like sales amount or customer demographics, we could extend this to analyze profitability or customer preferences across categories too."

2.21 SQL Query to Retrieve Customers Who Have Spent More Than $500.

```
SELECT CustomerID, SUM(TotalAmount) AS TotalSpent
FROM orders
GROUP BY CustomerID
HAVING SUM(TotalAmount) > 500;
```

■ How to Explain This in a Data Analyst Interview

"To identify customers who've spent more than $500, I used an aggregation query with SUM(TotalAmount) grouped by CustomerID. After computing each customer's total spend, I applied a HAVING clause to filter out only those whose total is above the $500 threshold.

This is a classic case of customer segmentation. For example, customers like **C001**, **C002**, and **C004** qualify as high-value customers based on their total spend.

Understanding high-spending customers is key for businesses—it helps with loyalty campaigns, special discounts, and personalized recommendations. If more data was available, I could layer this with purchase frequency or product preferences to refine the analysis."

2.22 SQL Query to Retrieve Get the Average Order Value for Each Customer.

```
SELECT CustomerID, AVG(TotalAmount) AS AvgOrderValue
FROM orders
GROUP BY CustomerID;
```

■How to Explain This in a Data Analyst Interview
"To calculate the average order value for each customer, I used the AVG() function on the TotalAmount, grouped by CustomerID. This gives me a clear picture of each customer's average spend per transaction.

For example, **Customer C001** has placed two orders totaling ₹500, which averages to ₹250 per order. Similarly, **Customer C003** placed one high-value order of ₹600.

This metric is important because average order value (AOV) helps businesses evaluate customer value and optimize their pricing and marketing strategies. If combined with frequency and recency data, we could also perform RFM (Recency-Frequency-Monetary) analysis for more advanced customer segmentation."

2.23 SQL Query to Retrieve the Percentage Contribution of Each Product to Total Sales.

```
SELECT
  ProductID,
  ProductName,
  SUM(SaleAmount) AS TotalProductSales,
  ROUND(SUM(SaleAmount) * 100.0 / (SELECT SUM(SaleAmount) FROM sales), 2) AS
PercentageContribution
FROM sales
GROUP BY ProductID, ProductName
ORDER BY PercentageContribution DESC;
```

■How to Explain This in a Data Analyst Interview
"In this case, I wanted to understand which products are driving our sales the most. I used a combination of aggregation (SUM) and a subquery to calculate each product's total sales as a percentage of all sales.

For instance, **Bluetooth Speakers (P002)** contributed the highest with **34.78%** of total sales. This indicates they're likely high performers, which could influence decisions like marketing spend, stock prioritization, or bundling strategies.

This kind of percentage-based analysis helps stakeholders quickly see the relative importance of each product, making it easier to identify star performers or underperformers in the product line."

2.24 SQL Query to Retrieve Customers Who Have Placed an Order But Never Returned.

We want to **find customers who placed orders**, but **none of their orders** were marked as Returned.

```
SELECT DISTINCT CustomerID
FROM orders
WHERE CustomerID NOT IN (
    SELECT DISTINCT CustomerID
    FROM orders
    WHERE ReturnStatus = 'Returned'
);
```

■How to Explain This in a Data Analyst Interview

"To find customers who have placed orders but never returned anything, I used a NOT IN subquery. First, I identified all customers who ever had a return (ReturnStatus = 'Returned'). Then, I excluded those from the list of all customers who placed an order.

For example, **C001**, **C003**, and **C005** placed at least one order, but none of their transactions were marked as returned.

This insight is particularly useful in customer loyalty or satisfaction analysis. These customers might be considered low-risk, potentially more loyal, or more likely to provide positive feedback. In a real-world scenario, I'd recommend targeting them with loyalty rewards or surveys to better understand their experience."

2.25 SQL Query to Retrieve the Highest-Selling Product in Each Month.

We want to group sales by **month**, sum the **sales per product**, and then select the **top-selling product** for each month.

```
WITH MonthlyProductSales AS (
  SELECT
    DATE_TRUNC('month', SaleDate) AS Month,
    ProductID,
    ProductName,
    SUM(SaleAmount) AS TotalSales
  FROM sales
  GROUP BY DATE_TRUNC('month', SaleDate), ProductID, ProductName
),
RankedSales AS (
  SELECT *,
    RANK() OVER (PARTITION BY Month ORDER BY TotalSales DESC) AS sales_rank
  FROM MonthlyProductSales
)
SELECT Month, ProductID, ProductName, TotalSales
FROM RankedSales
WHERE sales_rank = 1;
```

■ How to Explain This in a Data Analyst Interview
"To identify the top-performing product for each month, I used a CTE (Common Table Expression) to calculate total sales per product per month. Then, I applied a window function (RANK() OVER PARTITION BY Month) to rank the products based on their monthly sales.

For example, in January, the Bluetooth Speaker was the top-selling item with ₹500 in sales. In March, the Keyboard led with ₹600.

This type of analysis is really useful when you're trying to spot seasonal bestsellers, allocate marketing budgets efficiently, or make stock planning decisions. It shows how we can layer SQL logic to get both macro (monthly) and micro (product-level) insights from raw sales data."

2.26 SQL Query to Count the Number of Employees per Job Role.

Count how many employees are assigned to each **distinct job role**.

```
SELECT
  JobRole,
  COUNT(*) AS NumberOfEmployees
FROM employees
GROUP BY JobRole
ORDER BY NumberOfEmployees DESC;
```

■ How to Explain This in a Data Analyst Interview
> "To understand workforce composition, I grouped the employees table by JobRole and counted how many people are in each role. This is a very common aggregation task, often used by HR or operations to track hiring trends or team sizes.
> For instance, I found that we have **2 Data Analysts** and **2 Software Engineers**, indicating a balanced hiring trend across tech roles. This insight can help leaders determine if we're under-resourced in specific areas like data science or support.
> From a data analyst's perspective, it also opens the door for more complex questions — like team performance by job role, attrition by role, or even salary benchmarking. It's a great example of how simple groupings can generate valuable business intelligence."

2.27 SQL Query to Retrieve All Orders Where the Discount Applied Is Greater Than 20%.

We want to retrieve **only those orders** where the discount applied was **greater than 20%**

```
SELECT *
FROM orders
WHERE "Discount (%)" > 20;
```

■ How to Explain This in a Data Analyst Interview
> "To retrieve high-discount orders, I filtered the orders table using a simple WHERE clause on the Discount column. I set the condition to show only rows where the discount is greater than 20%.
> From the output, you can see that three orders qualify — for instance, **Order 103** had a 30% discount, and **Order 105** had 22%.
>
> This kind of analysis helps the business understand how often deep discounts are used and whether they're concentrated around certain customers, products, or time periods. It could also signal potential revenue leakage or the effectiveness of promotional strategies.
> As a data analyst, once I isolate these orders, I'd consider analyzing how these deep discounts impact overall profit margins or if they result in higher repeat purchase rates."

2.28 SQL Query to Get All Orders Placed on a Weekend.

SQL Query (for PostgreSQL / MySQL)

```
SELECT *
FROM orders
WHERE DAYOFWEEK(OrderDate) IN (1, 7);
```

In MySQL, DAYOFWEEK() returns 1 for Sunday, 7 for Saturday.

In PostgreSQL, use:

```
WHERE EXTRACT(DOW FROM OrderDate) IN (0, 6);
-- 0 = Sunday, 6 = Saturday
```

■How to Explain This in a Data Analyst Interview
"In this query, I wanted to find out which orders were placed during weekends, as it's important for identifying customer behavior patterns. I used the DAYOFWEEK() function to extract the weekday from the OrderDate, and filtered the results for Saturdays and Sundays. As shown, **Order 202** (placed on a Saturday) and **Order 203** (Sunday) are examples of weekend orders. This kind of insight could help teams schedule social media campaigns or discount offers when users are more active.

It also gives operations teams data to plan for potential weekend workload spikes, ensuring inventory and logistics are aligned. These little time-based patterns often lead to big optimizations in customer satisfaction and sales strategy."

2.29 SQL Query to Get All Orders Placed on a Weekend.

Determine which payment method has been used **most frequently**.

```
SELECT
  PaymentMethod,
  COUNT(*) AS UsageCount
FROM orders
GROUP BY PaymentMethod
ORDER BY UsageCount DESC
LIMIT 1;
```

■How to Explain This in a Data Analyst Interview
"To find out the most popular payment method among our customers, I grouped the orders by the PaymentMethod column and counted the number of times each method was used. From this analysis, I discovered that **Credit Card** was the top choice, used in 3 out of 6 transactions. This insight can help us ensure a smooth experience for credit card users and possibly prioritize this option in the checkout flow.

Also, from a business standpoint, knowing payment method popularity helps in negotiating better transaction rates with payment providers and even planning loyalty offers. For example, if UPI is growing fast, we can encourage more adoption by offering a discount on UPI payments.
This type of question may look simple, but it often connects directly to product design, finance, and user experience—so the insights can have a big impact across departments."

2.30 SQL Query to Find the Longest-Serving Employee in Each Department.

Find the employee with the **earliest JoinDate** in each department — i.e., the longest-serving employee.

```
SELECT Department, Name, MIN(JoinDate) AS FirstJoined
FROM employees
GROUP BY Department;
```

Or, to include the full employee details:

```
SELECT e.Department, e.Name, e.JoinDate
```

```
FROM employees e
INNER JOIN (
  SELECT Department, MIN(JoinDate) AS EarliestDate
  FROM employees
  GROUP BY Department
) sub
ON e.Department = sub.Department AND e.JoinDate = sub.EarliestDate;
```

■How to Explain This in a Data Analyst Interview

"This query helps us identify the longest-serving employee in each department by comparing the JoinDate values. I used a subquery to find the **minimum JoinDate per department**, and then joined it back to the main table to retrieve the actual employee names.

For example, in the Sales department, **John** has been with the company since **2013**, making him the most experienced in that team. Insights like these are helpful for HR when it comes to employee recognition, succession planning, or allocating responsibilities that require deep institutional knowledge.

This kind of problem also shows an understanding of both aggregate functions and joining techniques, which are key in SQL-based data analysis."

Solutions to Intermediate Level Questions

2.31 SQL Query to Find the top 5 highest-grossing movies.

SQL Query:

```
SELECT Title, Revenue
FROM movies
ORDER BY Revenue DESC
LIMIT 5;
```

■How to Explain This in a Data Analyst Interview
To find the top 5 highest-grossing movies, I first referred to the movies table, which included attributes like movie title, release year, and revenue.
Since we were interested in identifying movies that earned the most, I used a simple ORDER BY clause on the Revenue column in descending order, so that the highest-earning titles come first. I then used LIMIT 5 to restrict the result to only the top five.
From the output, 'Infinity Quest' led the box office with a revenue of $1045 million, followed by 'Titan Reign' and 'Skyfall Returns'.
This type of query is common in media analytics and business performance dashboards. It helps stakeholders understand which content or product performed best in monetary terms. It also showcases my ability to rank data and extract top performers — a valuable skill when working with KPIs, sales, or revenue datasets."

2.32 SQL Query to Calculate the total revenue generated per country.

SQL Query:

```
SELECT Country, SUM(Revenue) AS TotalRevenue
FROM sales
GROUP BY Country;
```

■How to Explain This in a Data Analyst Interview
"In this task, I was asked to calculate how much revenue was generated by each country. This is a common scenario in regional performance tracking or international sales reporting.
I worked with a dataset called sales, which included fields like Country, Product, and Revenue. To get the desired output, I used the SUM() aggregation function to total up all revenue per country and paired that with a GROUP BY clause based on the country column.
The query revealed that the **USA generated $2,100**, **Germany $2,050**, and **Canada $600** in total revenue. This kind of insight helps business teams decide where to focus more marketing efforts or supply chain investment.
What this shows is not just proficiency with SQL, but also the ability to translate data into business impact — a crucial trait for any data analyst."

2.33 SQL Query to Retrieve the first purchase date for each customer.

```
SELECT CustomerID, MIN(PurchaseDate) AS FirstPurchaseDate
FROM orders
GROUP BY CustomerID;
```

■How to Explain This in a Data Analyst Interview
To find the first purchase date per customer, I worked with the orders table which included customer IDs

and the corresponding purchase dates.

Since we needed to find the **earliest transaction date** for each customer, I used the MIN() function on the PurchaseDate column, grouped by CustomerID.

The result gave me exactly what we needed — for example, customer C002 placed their first order on **Jan 10, 2023**, and C004 on **March 5, 2023**.

This kind of query is very useful for **customer lifecycle analysis** or understanding **user onboarding behavior**. It can help businesses segment users based on how long they've been active and target them accordingly with personalized offers or retention campaigns.

What I love about this task is how a simple aggregation can give you really meaningful insight about customer behavior from the start

2.34 SQL Query to Find customers who have purchased more than 5 different products.

```
SELECT CustomerID, COUNT(DISTINCT ProductID) AS UniqueProducts
FROM orders
GROUP BY CustomerID
HAVING COUNT(DISTINCT ProductID) > 5;
```

■How to Explain This in a Data Analyst Interview

In this analysis, I was asked to identify high-engagement customers — specifically those who've bought more than 5 different products.

I used the orders table which tracks each customer's purchases, including the product ID and order details. To determine how many different products each customer bought, I used COUNT(DISTINCT ProductID) and grouped the results by CustomerID.

To filter out only those with more than 5 distinct products, I applied the HAVING clause. The result showed that customer C001 had purchased 6 unique products, making them a strong potential for loyalty or upsell campaigns.

This kind of analysis is really valuable for customer segmentation — helping the business distinguish between one-time buyers and those who show broad product interest. It can drive smarter marketing and personalized product recommendations.

2.35 SQL Query to Retrieve employees who have more than 5 years of experience.

```
SELECT EmployeeID, Name, Department, JoinDate,
       DATEDIFF(YEAR, JoinDate, '2025-04-04') AS YearsOfExperience
FROM employees
WHERE DATEDIFF(YEAR, JoinDate, '2025-04-04') > 5;
```

Note: DATEDIFF() syntax varies slightly in different SQL dialects — this works in T-SQL (SQL Server). In MySQL, you might need to use TIMESTAMPDIFF(YEAR, JoinDate, CURDATE()).

■How to Explain This in a Data Analyst Interview

To retrieve employees with more than 5 years of experience, I referred to the employees table, focusing on their JoinDate.

Using a date difference function (DATEDIFF), I calculated how many full years have passed between their join date and today's date. Then I applied a filter (WHERE clause) to include only those with more than 5 years.

For instance, **Rakesh Yadav**, who joined back in 2010, has been with the company for **14 years**, while **Meena Gupta** has 7 years of experience. This kind of data is super useful for **retention analysis**, **seniority-based promotions**, or simply tracking **organizational loyalty**.

This task really emphasizes how valuable even a simple date field can be when analyzed effectively.

2.36 SQL Query to Get all transactions where the total amount is greater than twice the average order value.

Step-by-Step Approach:

To answer this, we first need to:
1. Calculate the average order value from the entire orders table.
2. Multiply it by 2 to get our threshold.
3. Retrieve orders whose TotalAmount exceeds this threshold.

Let's first compute the average order value:

```
(150 + 400 + 250 + 100 + 300 + 800) / 6 = 333.33
Twice the average = 666.66
```

```
SELECT *
FROM orders
WHERE TotalAmount > (
    SELECT AVG(TotalAmount) * 2
    FROM orders
);
```

■How to Explain This in a Data Analyst Interview
In this task, I wanted to flag unusually large transactions — specifically, any order whose total value was greater than twice the average order value.
I started by calculating the average value of all orders using an aggregate function (AVG(TotalAmount)). Once I had that value, I multiplied it by 2 to set the benchmark threshold.
Then, using a subquery inside my WHERE clause, I filtered the orders table to only return those entries where TotalAmount exceeded this dynamic benchmark.
In this dataset, only one transaction stood out — Order O006, with a value of 800, which is significantly higher than the average. This approach is really helpful in identifying outlier transactions — which can be used for fraud detection, VIP customer tagging, or inventory impact analysis.
I love problems like this because they combine aggregation with subquery logic — helping reveal insights that aren't visible with raw totals alone

2.37 SQL Query to Retrieve the products that have never been sold.

```
SELECT ProductID, ProductName, Category
FROM products
WHERE ProductID NOT IN (
    SELECT DISTINCT ProductID FROM order_items
);
```

■How to Explain This in a Data Analyst Interview
In this case, my goal was to identify products that are listed in the inventory but have never been purchased — meaning they've never appeared in any transaction record.
I used a subquery to extract all unique ProductIDs from the order_items table — this represents all products that have been sold at least once. Then I applied a NOT IN filter on the products table to exclude those and keep only the products that haven't been sold.
From the sample data, the 'Yoga Mat' and 'Laptop Sleeve' are two such products — they exist in our catalog but haven't been part of any sale yet.

This kind of insight is super useful for identifying dead stock or products that might need better promotion, discounts, or even removal from the catalog. It's a great example of how SQL can help align sales data with inventory planning and marketing strategy.

2.38 SQL Query to Find the month with the highest revenue.

Step-by-Step Thinking:
1. Extract the **month** from the OrderDate column.
2. **Group** orders by month.
3. **Sum** the TotalAmount for each group.
4. Retrieve the month with the **maximum revenue**.

```
SELECT
    TO_CHAR(OrderDate, 'YYYY-MM') AS OrderMonth,
    SUM(TotalAmount) AS TotalRevenue
FROM orders
GROUP BY TO_CHAR(OrderDate, 'YYYY-MM')
ORDER BY TotalRevenue DESC
LIMIT 1;
```

(If using MySQL, you could use DATE_FORMAT(OrderDate, '%Y-%m') instead.)

■How to Explain This in a Data Analyst Interview
To identify the month that generated the highest revenue, I began by extracting the month component from the OrderDate column using a date formatting function. Then, I used the SUM() function to aggregate the total revenue per month.
After grouping the data, I ordered the results in descending order of revenue and picked the top result using LIMIT 1.
From the dataset, I found that February 2024 generated the highest revenue of 1400. This kind of monthly breakdown is super valuable in business contexts — it helps stakeholders spot seasonal patterns, evaluate campaign impacts, and make budget decisions.
In real-world scenarios, I'd also consider slicing this by category, customer segment, or region for deeper insights.

2.39 SQL Query to Retrieve customers who have purchased the same product more than once.

Step-by-Step Thought Process:
1. Group the data by both **CustomerID** and **ProductID**.
2. Count how many times the same customer bought the **same product**.
3. Filter out only those where the count is greater than 1 — meaning the same product was bought more than once by the same customer.

```
SELECT
    CustomerID,
    ProductID,
    COUNT(*) AS PurchaseCount
FROM OrderDetails
GROUP BY CustomerID, ProductID
HAVING COUNT(*) > 1;
```

■How to Explain This in a Data Analyst Interview

To identify customers who purchased the same product more than once, I started by grouping the data by CustomerID and ProductID. This way, I could analyze purchases on a per-customer, per-product basis. Then I used the COUNT(*) function to count the number of times a product was ordered by a customer. Finally, I applied a HAVING clause to filter only those combinations where the count was greater than one.

From our dataset, we can see that:
- Customer C001 purchased product P101 twice.
- Customer C002 purchased product P102 twice.

This kind of analysis is especially helpful in customer retention or upsell strategies. For example, customers repeatedly buying the same item might be interested in bulk purchase offers or loyalty rewards. Also, it can help businesses forecast inventory for high-repeat items

2.40 SQL Query to Count the number of distinct product categories sold each month.

Step-by-Step Thought Process:
1. Join Orders, OrderDetails, and Products to connect order dates with product categories.
2. Extract the month from the OrderDate.
3. Group the data by month.
4. Count the number of distinct product categories sold in that month.

```
SELECT
    TO_CHAR(o.OrderDate, 'YYYY-MM') AS Month,
    COUNT(DISTINCT p.Category) AS DistinctCategoriesSold
FROM Orders o
JOIN OrderDetails od ON o.OrderID = od.OrderID
JOIN Products p ON od.ProductID = p.ProductID
GROUP BY TO_CHAR(o.OrderDate, 'YYYY-MM')
ORDER BY Month;
```

■How to Explain This in a Data Analyst Interview
To calculate how many distinct product categories were sold each month, I began by joining the Orders, OrderDetails, and Products tables so I could link each order with its product and corresponding category. Then, I extracted the month from the OrderDate using the TO_CHAR() function. This allowed me to group the data by month.

Within each month, I used COUNT(DISTINCT category) to ensure we're not just counting the number of products, but specifically how many different categories were sold.

For instance, in January 2024, we sold products from 2 categories — Electronics and Clothing. In February, we expanded to include Home Decor as well, so we had 3 distinct categories that month.

This metric is really useful when evaluating product variety across time — especially for tracking diversification, seasonal performance, or inventory planning.

2.41 SQL Query to Find all customers who have placed orders in more than one country.

```
SELECT
    c.CustomerID,
    c.Name
FROM Customers c
JOIN Orders o ON c.CustomerID = o.CustomerID
GROUP BY c.CustomerID, c.Name
HAVING COUNT(DISTINCT o.Country) > 1;
```

■How to Explain This in a Data Analyst Interview
To identify customers who've placed orders in **multiple countries**, I started by joining the Customers and Orders tables. The goal was to associate each order with the customer and the country where the order was placed.
Then I grouped the data by customer and used COUNT(DISTINCT Country) to count the number of **unique countries** each customer has ordered from.
Finally, I used the HAVING clause to filter for only those customers where this count was more than one. For example, Alice placed orders in both the USA and Canada, and Ethan placed orders in Germany and France — so they meet the criteria. This kind of insight is super useful in understanding cross-border buying behavior, which can help shape global marketing or logistics strategies.

2.42 SQL Query to Calculate the moving average of monthly sales.

If this data were in a SQL table called MonthlySales, here's a way you might write it (in a SQL dialect that supports window functions):

```
SELECT
    Month,
    Sales,
    ROUND(AVG(Sales) OVER (
        ORDER BY Month
        ROWS BETWEEN 2 PRECEDING AND CURRENT ROW
    ), 2) AS Moving_Avg
FROM MonthlySales;
```

■How to Explain This in a Data Analyst Interview
To calculate the **3-month moving average of monthly sales**, I began with a table that includes sales figures for each month. A moving average helps us **smooth out seasonal spikes or dips** and get a better picture of the underlying trend.
Since a 3-month moving average considers the current month and the two before it, I applied a rolling window logic. For instance, to calculate April's moving average, I averaged sales from February, March, and April.
In SQL, this is handled cleanly using **window functions**, specifically AVG() with ROWS BETWEEN 2 PRECEDING AND CURRENT ROW. This gives us a dynamic moving average for each month after the first two.
This kind of analysis is especially useful for forecasting, identifying slowdowns or surges, and setting more data-driven targets for upcoming months.

2.43 SQL Query to Retrieve the top 3 highest revenue-generating regions.

Step 1: Calculate Revenue = Quantity × Price
Let's first add the revenue column:

Order_ID	Region	Product	Quantity	Price	Revenue
101	North	Laptop	2	800	1600
102	South	Phone	3	300	900
103	East	Headphones	5	50	250
104	West	Laptop	1	800	800

| 105 | North | Phone | 4 | 300 | 1200 |
| 106 | South | Laptop | 1 | 800 | 800 |

Step 2: Group by Region and Sum Revenue

Region	Total_Revenue
North	2800
South	1700
East	250
West	800

Final Output: Top 3 Revenue-Generating Regions

Rank	Region	Total_Revenue
1	North	2800
2	South	1700
3	West	800

```
SELECT
    Region,
    SUM(Quantity * Price) AS Total_Revenue
FROM Sales
GROUP BY Region
ORDER BY Total_Revenue DESC
LIMIT 3;
```

■How to Explain This in a Data Analyst Interview
To identify the top 3 revenue-generating regions, I first ensured I had a dataset with quantity and price for each order. I calculated revenue per transaction using Quantity × Price. Then, I grouped the data by region and summed up the revenue to get total earnings for each.
Once I had total revenue by region, I sorted the results in descending order to find the top contributors. The top 3 in this case were North, South, and West.
This kind of analysis is really important for business stakeholders to understand where their biggest markets are geographically and where to focus their marketing or logistics efforts. In SQL, I'd use GROUP BY and ORDER BY, combined with a LIMIT to retrieve the top performers.

2.44 SQL Query to Get the highest-rated products in each category.

```
SELECT Category, Product_Name, Rating
FROM Products p
WHERE Rating = (
    SELECT MAX(Rating)
    FROM Products
    WHERE Category = p.Category
```

```
);
```

How to Explain This in a Data Analyst Interview
To determine the highest-rated products in each category, I first grouped the products based on their categories—like Electronics, Beauty, and Footwear. Within each group, I identified the maximum rating using aggregation.

But just finding the maximum rating isn't enough. I had to match those max ratings back to the specific product names, which is where filtering with a subquery or using RANK() or ROW_NUMBER() also comes in handy if there are ties.

This kind of insight is extremely valuable when presenting best-sellers or recommending top products per segment on e-commerce platforms. It helps marketing teams highlight top-rated products, and it also improves customer trust when they see what's most loved in each category.

2.45 SQL Query to Find employees who have referred more than 3 other employees.

Step-by-Step Logic:
1. Objective: Identify employees who are *referrers* — i.e., their Employee_ID appears in the Referred_By column.
2. Group and Count: We group the data by Referred_By and count how many times each ID appears.
3. Apply Filter: Filter only those with a count greater than 3.
4. Join for Names (optional): If needed, we can join this result back to the Employees table to retrieve the name of the referrer.

```
SELECT e.Employee_ID AS Referrer_ID, e.Name, COUNT(*) AS Referral_Count
FROM Employees AS r
JOIN Employees AS e
  ON r.Referred_By = e.Employee_ID
GROUP BY e.Employee_ID, e.Name
HAVING COUNT(*) > 3;
```

How to Explain This in a Data Analyst Interview
To solve this, I looked at the Referred_By column, which tracks who referred each employee. I treated that column like a reverse relationship—so instead of seeing who was referred, I used it to identify who did the referring.

I grouped the data by Referred_By, and counted how many employees each person brought in. Then I filtered to only include those who referred more than 3 employees. In our dataset, Alice stands out as a super-referrer with 4 hires under her name.

This kind of analysis is valuable for understanding employee advocacy and even HR incentive programs. If a particular employee is bringing in high-quality referrals, they could be recognized or rewarded appropriately. Plus, from a people analytics perspective, this helps us see who's contributing to the company's growth beyond just their daily work.

2.46 SQL Query to Retrieve orders that contain multiple products.

```
SELECT Order_ID, COUNT(Product_ID) AS Product_Count
FROM OrderDetails
GROUP BY Order_ID
HAVING COUNT(Product_ID) > 1;
```

■How to Explain This in a Data Analyst Interview

To identify orders containing multiple products, I analyzed the OrderDetails table where each row represents a line item in an order. My goal was to find orders that had more than one distinct product associated with them.

I grouped the data by Order_ID and counted the number of product entries for each. Orders with a product count greater than one were flagged as multi-product orders. In our example dataset, orders 201 and 203 had more than one product each.

This type of analysis is particularly useful in understanding customer behavior. For instance, customers placing multi-product orders may indicate higher intent or better engagement, which could help with segmenting high-value customers or shaping upselling strategies.

2.47 SQL Query to Count the number of users who have logged in more than 5 times in a month.

Step-by-Step Logic:
1. Extract Month and Year from the Login_Date to group logins monthly.
2. Group by User_ID and Month-Year.
3. Count logins per user per month.
4. Filter those with more than 5 logins in the month.
5. Count distinct users who meet that condition.

```sql
SELECT COUNT(DISTINCT User_ID) AS Active_Users
FROM (
    SELECT User_ID, DATE_FORMAT(Login_Date, '%Y-%m') AS Month, COUNT(*) AS
Login_Count
    FROM UserLogins
    GROUP BY User_ID, Month
    HAVING COUNT(*) > 5
) AS MonthlyLogins;
```

■How to Explain This in a Data Analyst Interview

To count the number of users logging in more than 5 times within a month, I first grouped the login data by User_ID and extracted the month and year from each login date. This allowed me to track login activity on a monthly basis.

Then, I calculated the login count per user per month using an aggregate function. Finally, I filtered the result to include only users whose login frequency exceeded 5 within that time period. In the sample dataset, 2 users—U001 and U003—logged in more than 5 times during March 2024.

This kind of metric is really helpful for understanding user engagement. Users who log in frequently are typically more active, so tracking this helps product and growth teams make informed decisions about customer retention strategies.

2.48 SQL Query to Find the percentage of repeat customers.

Step-by-Step Logic:
1. Group the data by Customer_ID and count the number of orders per customer.
2. Define repeat customers as those who have placed more than 1 order.
3. Calculate total customers and total repeat customers.
4. Divide repeat customers by total customers and multiply by 100 to get the percentage.

```sql
SELECT
  ROUND(
    (COUNT(*) FILTER (WHERE TotalOrders > 1) * 100.0) / COUNT(*), 2
```

```
    ) AS RepeatCustomerPercentage
FROM (
    SELECT Customer_ID, COUNT(*) AS TotalOrders
    FROM Orders
    GROUP BY Customer_ID
) AS CustomerOrders;
```

■How to Explain This in a Data Analyst Interview

To determine the percentage of repeat customers, I first grouped the orders by Customer_ID and calculated the number of orders each customer placed. A repeat customer is one who has placed more than one order.

After that, I calculated the total number of unique customers and counted how many had placed more than one order. In this dataset of 4 customers, 2 made repeat purchases, giving us a repeat customer rate of 50%.

This metric is valuable for understanding customer loyalty and retention. A higher repeat customer percentage often reflects strong customer satisfaction and can guide marketing teams on retention-focused campaigns.

2.49 SQL Query to Retrieve products that are priced in the top 10% of all products.

Step-by-Step Logic:
1. Sort the products by Price in descending order.
2. Calculate the 90th percentile (top 10%) price threshold.
3. Filter the products whose prices are greater than or equal to that threshold.

90th Percentile Calculation:
- Total Products = 10
- 90th Percentile Position = 90% × 10 = 9th product (in sorted order)

Sorted Prices (descending):

```
300, 220, 200, 150, 100, 80, 60, 40, 25, 20
```

- 90th percentile price = 220

```
SELECT *
FROM Products
WHERE Price >= (
  SELECT PERCENTILE_CONT(0.9) WITHIN GROUP (ORDER BY Price)
  FROM Products
);
```

■How to Explain This in a Data Analyst Interview

To identify products priced in the top 10%, I first sorted all products by price in descending order. Then, I calculated the 90th percentile threshold—since we want the top 10%, we look at the price above which the top 10% of products lie.

In this dataset of 10 products, the 90th percentile price came out to $220. So, any product priced at $220 or higher qualifies. Two products—'Luxury Leather Bag' and 'High-end Sunglasses'—met this criteria. This type of analysis is useful in pricing strategies, understanding premium product ranges, and targeting high-value inventory in marketing or inventory forecasting.

2.50 SQL Query to Find the city with the most orders placed.

Step-by-step Breakdown:
1. Group the data by City.
2. Count the number of orders per city.
3. Identify the city with the highest count.

```
SELECT City, COUNT(Order_ID) AS Number_of_Orders
FROM Orders
GROUP BY City
ORDER BY Number_of_Orders DESC
LIMIT 1;
```

◼How to Explain This in a Data Analyst Interview
To determine which city had the highest order volume, I grouped the data by City and counted the number of orders for each. This aggregation allowed me to compare performance across different locations.
In this case, **Mumbai** stood out with 3 orders, followed by Delhi and Bangalore. So, Mumbai is the city with the most orders placed.
This kind of insight is valuable for operations and marketing—it helps the business identify key geographies to focus promotions, manage inventory, or plan delivery logistics.

2.51 SQL Query to Retrieve all customers who have ordered more than the average order value.

Step-by-Step Logic
1. Calculate the average order value:
   - Add all order values: 200 + 450 + 300 + 150 + 500 + 100 = 1700
   - Total number of orders: 6
   - Average Order Value = 1700 / 6 = ~283.33
2. Filter customers whose order value is greater than 283.33.

```
SELECT Customer_ID, Order_Value
FROM Orders
WHERE Order_Value > (
    SELECT AVG(Order_Value) FROM Orders
);
```

◼How to Explain This in a Data Analyst Interview
To identify customers who ordered more than the average order value, I first calculated the overall average from the Order_Value field. In this case, the average was approximately $283. I then filtered the dataset to retrieve only those customers whose order exceeded that benchmark.
This kind of analysis is useful in customer segmentation. High-value customers can be targeted with loyalty programs or premium offers to drive retention and additional revenue.
I usually prefer embedding such logic into a subquery, which makes the query dynamic and scalable as new data comes in.

2.52 SQL Query to Find products that are frequently purchased together.

```
SELECT
    od1.ProductID AS ProductA,
```

```
    od2.ProductID AS ProductB,
    COUNT(*) AS TimesBoughtTogether
FROM
    OrderDetails od1
JOIN
    OrderDetails od2
    ON od1.OrderID = od2.OrderID AND od1.ProductID < od2.ProductID
GROUP BY
    od1.ProductID, od2.ProductID
HAVING
    COUNT(*) >= 2
ORDER BY
    TimesBoughtTogether DESC;
```

■ How to Explain This in a Data Analyst Interview

To analyze frequently purchased product combinations, I focused on the OrderDetails table, which tracks which products were part of which orders. The logic is simple: if two products appear in the same order, they were purchased together.

I used a self-join on the OrderDetails table to match each product in an order with every other product in the same order. To avoid duplicate or reverse combinations (like P101–P102 vs. P102–P101), I added a condition so that ProductID1 < ProductID2.

Then, I grouped the results by these product pairs and counted how many times each pair appeared across all orders. By adding a HAVING COUNT(*) >= 2, I filtered to only the meaningful combinations that appeared together at least twice.

In this dataset, I found that 'Coffee Beans' and 'French Press' were bought together in 3 separate orders, which is a strong signal that customers tend to buy them as a pair.

This kind of insight is extremely valuable for product bundling, personalized recommendations, or even designing targeted promotions. For example, if a customer adds Coffee Beans to their cart, we can recommend a French Press based on this behavior.

2.53 SQL Query to Retrieve customers who have the highest lifetime value.

```
SELECT
    c.CustomerID,
    c.CustomerName,
    SUM(od.Quantity * od.UnitPrice) AS LifetimeValue
FROM
    Customers c
JOIN
    Orders o ON c.CustomerID = o.CustomerID
JOIN
    OrderDetails od ON o.OrderID = od.OrderID
GROUP BY
    c.CustomerID, c.CustomerName
ORDER BY
    LifetimeValue DESC
LIMIT 1;
```

■ How to Explain This in a Data Analyst Interview

To find the customer with the highest lifetime value, I first clarified what 'lifetime value' means in this context — typically, it's the total revenue generated by a customer across all their purchases.
I began by joining the Customers, Orders, and OrderDetails tables so I could trace every product each customer has purchased. Then, for each item in an order, I multiplied Quantity * UnitPrice to get the revenue for that line item.
After that, I grouped the data by CustomerID and CustomerName and summed up the revenue per customer. Finally, I sorted the result in descending order of lifetime value and used LIMIT 1 to get the top customer.
In this case, Alice (C001) came out on top with a lifetime value of 1050, based on her purchases across 3 different orders.
This kind of analysis is extremely helpful in marketing — we can target our top customers with loyalty programs, personalized offers, or early access to new products. It's also a great foundation for customer segmentation or churn prediction models.

2.54 SQL Query to Find employees who have the highest number of direct reports.

```
SELECT
    e.EmployeeID,
    e.Name AS ManagerName,
    COUNT(r.EmployeeID) AS DirectReports
FROM
    Employees e
LEFT JOIN
    Employees r ON e.EmployeeID = r.ManagerID
GROUP BY
    e.EmployeeID, e.Name
ORDER BY
    DirectReports DESC
LIMIT 1;
```

■How to Explain This in a Data Analyst Interview
To identify the employee with the highest number of direct reports, I used a self-join on the Employees table.
The idea is simple: each employee has a ManagerID that references the EmployeeID of their manager. So, I joined the table to itself where e.EmployeeID = r.ManagerID — this means we're matching each manager with their direct reports.
Then, I grouped the data by each manager and counted how many employees report to them directly. Finally, I sorted by the count of direct reports in descending order and used LIMIT 1 to get the manager with the most direct reports.
In this case, Alice (E001) has 3 direct reports — Bob, Charlie, and Ethan — making her the top-level manager with the most direct responsibility.
This kind of insight is helpful when analyzing organizational hierarchy, team structure, or for identifying managers under the heaviest workload, which can guide HR decisions or workforce planning.

2.55 SQL Query to Retrieve all transactions where the total amount exceeds the 90th percentile.

SQL Query (Using PERCENTILE_CONT — works in PostgreSQL, SQL Server, Oracle)

```
WITH PercentileCTE AS (
    SELECT
        PERCENTILE_CONT(0.9) WITHIN GROUP (ORDER BY Amount) AS percentile_90
```

```
    FROM
        Transactions
)

SELECT
    t.*
FROM
    Transactions t
JOIN
    PercentileCTE p ON t.Amount > p.percentile_90;
```

Explanation of 90th Percentile Logic:
Sorted Amounts: **100, 180, 220, 250, 400, 600**
- 90th percentile = value **greater than or equal to 90%** of the rest
- In this case, it's roughly **between 400 and 600**, so we retrieve any amount **greater than 90th percentile** → Only 600

■How to Explain This in a Data Analyst Interview
To retrieve all transactions where the total amount exceeds the 90th percentile, I first needed to calculate what the 90th percentile amount actually is.
I used the PERCENTILE_CONT window function, which helps identify the continuous percentile value from a dataset — in this case, from the Amount column in the Transactions table.
After calculating that value inside a common table expression (CTE), I joined it back to the Transactions table and filtered for rows where the amount is greater than that percentile.
In this dataset, the 90th percentile fell between 400 and 600, so only the transaction with an amount of 600 was above that threshold.
This technique is super useful for spotting outlier or high-value transactions — ideal for fraud detection, VIP customer targeting, or optimizing marketing spend.
Plus, by using a CTE, I kept the logic clean and readable for future use or reporting.

2.56 SQL Query to Retrieve all transactions where the total amount exceeds the 90th percentile.

```
WITH OrderDifferences AS (
    SELECT
        CustomerID,
        OrderDate,
        LAG(OrderDate) OVER (PARTITION BY CustomerID ORDER BY OrderDate) AS
PreviousOrderDate
    FROM
        Orders
),
DateDiffs AS (
    SELECT
        CustomerID,
        DATEDIFF(DAY, PreviousOrderDate, OrderDate) AS DaysBetweenOrders
    FROM
        OrderDifferences
    WHERE
```

```
        PreviousOrderDate IS NOT NULL
)
SELECT
    CustomerID,
    AVG(DaysBetweenOrders) AS AvgDaysBetweenOrders
FROM
    DateDiffs
GROUP BY
    CustomerID;
```

Explanation of Logic:
We used a window function (LAG) to look at the previous order date per customer, then calculated the difference in days. Finally, we grouped by customer to get each customer's average gap between orders.

Breakdown:
- C001 orders: June 1 → June 5 → June 10
  - Gaps: 4 days, 5 days → Avg = (4+5)/2 = 4.5 (rounded as 4)
- C002 orders: June 2 → June 6
  - Gap: 4 days

■ How to Explain This in a Data Analyst Interview
To calculate the average time between customer orders, I started by using a window function — specifically LAG() — to compare each order date to the previous order for the same customer.
This helped me find how many days passed between each of their orders. Then I used DATEDIFF to calculate the difference in days between the current and previous order.
I filtered out nulls (because first orders don't have a 'previous'), and then I grouped the data by customer to find each person's average gap between purchases.
For example, Customer C001 placed 3 orders with gaps of 4 and 5 days, so their average reorder time was 4.5 days. This kind of insight is really useful for customer retention strategies, optimizing email reminders, or identifying churn risks.
In practice, I'd also look at this metric over time to see if reorder behavior is speeding up or slowing down across different customer segments.

2.57 Retrieve orders where the shipping time was longer than expected.

```
SELECT
    OrderID,
    CustomerID,
    OrderDate,
    ExpectedShipDate,
    ActualShipDate,
    DATEDIFF(DAY, ExpectedShipDate, ActualShipDate) AS DelayInDays
FROM
    Orders
WHERE
    ActualShipDate > ExpectedShipDate;
```

■ How to Explain This in a Data Analyst Interview
To identify orders where shipping took longer than expected, I compared the ActualShipDate with the ExpectedShipDate for each order.

I used a simple WHERE condition — ActualShipDate > ExpectedShipDate — to filter only those orders that were delayed.

Additionally, I used DATEDIFF to calculate how many days each shipment was late, which I included as a new column (DelayInDays) for clarity.

For example, Order 205 (Customer C005) was expected to ship by July 9 but was actually shipped on July 13, which is a 4-day delay.

This kind of query is super useful for tracking logistics performance, identifying bottlenecks in the supply chain, or reporting on customer experience impact.

If I were analyzing this deeper, I'd go on to segment delays by product category, shipping region, or vendor to pinpoint where improvements are needed.

2.58 Retrieve orders where the shipping time was longer than expected.

```
SELECT
    COUNT(DISTINCT UserID) AS UniqueVisitors
FROM
    WebsiteVisits;
```

Explanation:
Even though there are 6 visits in the table, only **4 unique users** visited:
- U001, U002, U003, U004

How to Explain This in a Data Analyst Interview
To count the number of unique visitors to an e-commerce site, I used the WebsiteVisits table and simply selected the count of distinct UserID values.

This ensures we're not double-counting users who visited multiple times — like User U001, who appears more than once but should only count as a single visitor.

The logic is clean: every row is a visit, but a unique visitor is identified by a unique user ID, so using COUNT(DISTINCT UserID) gives the accurate number of individual users.

This metric is critical for evaluating how many real users your platform is attracting, regardless of how active they are. If you're trying to measure reach, campaign performance, or new user acquisition, this is one of your core KPIs.

If needed, I could also break this down by day, week, or device to spot trends in user behavior over time.

2.59 Retrieve orders where the shipping time was longer than expected.

```
WITH BrandSales AS (
    SELECT
        ProductCategory,
        Brand,
        SUM(Quantity) AS TotalQuantity
    FROM
        Sales
    GROUP BY
        ProductCategory, Brand
),
RankedBrands AS (
    SELECT *,
            RANK() OVER (PARTITION BY ProductCategory ORDER BY TotalQuantity DESC)
AS RankInCategory
```

```
        FROM BrandSales
)
SELECT
    ProductCategory,
    Brand,
    TotalQuantity
FROM
    RankedBrands
WHERE
    RankInCategory = 1;
```

■How to Explain This in a Data Analyst Interview

To find the most purchased brand within each product category, I broke the solution into two logical steps using CTEs (Common Table Expressions).

First, I aggregated the total quantity sold per brand in each product category using SUM(Quantity) and a GROUP BY on ProductCategory and Brand. This gave me a clear view of which brand sold how much within its category.

Next, I used a **window function** — RANK() — partitioned by product category and ordered by total quantity in descending order. This assigned a rank to each brand based on how much they sold within their category.

Finally, I filtered to keep only the top-ranked brand (RANK() = 1) in each category — this gave me the most purchased brand per category.

For example, in the 'Clothing' category, Nike had a total of 10 units (6+4), but Adidas had 9 — oops! Actually, **Nike should win here**. Let's fix the dataset:

2.60 Find the revenue contribution of each sales representative.

```
WITH RevenueByRep AS (
    SELECT
        SalesRep,
        SUM(Revenue) AS TotalRevenue
    FROM Sales
    GROUP BY SalesRep
),
TotalRevenueSum AS (
    SELECT SUM(Revenue) AS OverallRevenue
    FROM Sales
)
SELECT
    r.SalesRep,
    r.TotalRevenue,
    ROUND((r.TotalRevenue * 100.0) / t.OverallRevenue, 2) AS
RevenueContributionPercent
FROM
    RevenueByRep r, TotalRevenueSum t;
```

■How to Explain This in a Data Analyst Interview

To find how much revenue each sales representative contributed to the overall sales, I broke the problem down into two steps:

First, I aggregated the revenue per SalesRep using SUM(Revenue) and grouped by SalesRep. This gave me total revenue handled by each individual.

Second, I calculated the total revenue across all reps, and then derived the contribution percentage by dividing each rep's total by the grand total. I used ROUND to keep it readable.

For example, Alice made ₹1600 in sales out of ₹3600 overall — which is ~44.44% of total sales.

This kind of analysis is super useful for evaluating individual sales performance, identifying top performers, and shaping commission models or territory assignments.

If I had more data like region or time period, I could extend this query to see how reps are doing monthly or in different markets.

2.61 Find the revenue contribution of each sales representative.

```
SELECT
    EmployeeID,
    EmployeeName,
    COUNT(DISTINCT Department) AS DepartmentCount
FROM
    EmployeeDepartmentHistory
GROUP BY
    EmployeeID, EmployeeName
HAVING
    COUNT(DISTINCT Department) > 1;
```

■How to Explain This in a Data Analyst Interview

To find employees who have worked in more than one department, I started with the EmployeeDepartmentHistory table, which tracks employee assignments over time.

I grouped the data by EmployeeID and EmployeeName, and counted the distinct departments they've worked in using COUNT(DISTINCT Department).

I then applied a HAVING clause to filter only those employees where this count is greater than 1 — which means they've switched departments or held cross-functional roles.

In this example, Alice worked in both HR and IT, and Bob transitioned from Finance to Marketing.

This kind of query is really useful in HR analytics or workforce planning — for identifying employees with diverse experience, cross-department exposure, or potential internal mobility candidates.

2.62 Find customers who have placed orders on their birthdays.

```
SELECT
    c.CustomerID,
    c.CustomerName,
    c.DOB,
    o.OrderID,
    o.OrderDate,
    o.Amount
FROM
    Customers c
JOIN
    Orders o
ON
    c.CustomerID = o.CustomerID
WHERE
```

```
EXTRACT(MONTH FROM c.DOB) = EXTRACT(MONTH FROM o.OrderDate)
AND EXTRACT(DAY FROM c.DOB) = EXTRACT(DAY FROM o.OrderDate);
```

■How to Explain This in a Data Analyst Interview
To find customers who placed an order on their birthday, I started by joining the Customers and Orders tables using CustomerID.
The key logic was to match the month and day of the customer's DOB with the OrderDate, which I extracted using EXTRACT(MONTH FROM ...) and EXTRACT(DAY FROM ...).
I didn't compare the full date (since year will always differ) — we only care if the order date falls on the same day and month as the customer's birthdate.
For instance, Alice (DOB: June 15) placed an order on June 15, 2023 — so she qualifies. Same for Carol.
This kind of query is very helpful in CRM or e-commerce settings, especially for designing personalized birthday offers, tracking customer loyalty, or running targeted campaigns.

2.63 Retrieve all orders where the payment method changed after checkout.

```
SELECT
    o.OrderID,
    o.CustomerID,
    o.CheckoutPaymentMethod,
    p.FinalPaymentMethod,
    p.PaymentDate
FROM
    Orders o
JOIN
    Payments p ON o.OrderID = p.OrderID
WHERE
    o.CheckoutPaymentMethod <> p.FinalPaymentMethod;
```

In this scenario, the business wants to identify any orders where the **customer chose a different payment method at final payment compared to what they selected during checkout**.
To solve this, I joined the Orders and Payments tables using OrderID. Then, I applied a WHERE clause to filter records where CheckoutPaymentMethod **does not equal** FinalPaymentMethod.
This highlights mismatches — for example, Order O1002 was supposed to be paid via **UPI**, but was finalized with a **Credit Card**.
These discrepancies might suggest:
- A change in user intent or available funds
- Possible **payment system issues**
- Or even **fraudulent or risky behavior** in some use cases

If I had timestamps, I could even check **how long after checkout** the method was changed. This would help in tracking delays or potential loopholes.

2.64 Find products that had the highest sales increase month over month.

```
WITH SalesWithGrowth AS (
    SELECT
        ProductID,
        ProductName,
```

```
        SaleMonth,
        TotalSales,
        LAG(TotalSales) OVER (PARTITION BY ProductID ORDER BY SaleMonth) AS
PrevMonthSales,
        (TotalSales - LAG(TotalSales) OVER (PARTITION BY ProductID ORDER BY
SaleMonth)) AS SalesGrowth
    FROM
        Sales
)
SELECT
    ProductID,
    ProductName,
    SaleMonth,
    TotalSales,
    PrevMonthSales,
    SalesGrowth
FROM
    SalesWithGrowth
WHERE
    SalesGrowth IS NOT NULL
ORDER BY
    SalesGrowth DESC
LIMIT 1;
```

To find which product had the **highest increase in sales month-over-month**, I used a window function with LAG() to fetch the **previous month's sales** for each product.

Then, I calculated the difference between the current and previous month's sales — calling that **SalesGrowth**.

After that, I simply filtered out rows where the growth is NULL (i.e., where there's no prior month), and sorted the results by SalesGrowth in descending order. The product with the top increase shows up at the top.

In this case, **Sneakers** had a major jump — from ₹1000 in Jan to ₹1800 in Feb, a net growth of ₹800, which was the highest among all.

This kind of query is crucial for identifying **fast-growing products**, planning **inventory**, or even preparing **campaigns for trending items**.

2.65 Find products that had the highest sales increase month over month.

```
SELECT
    COUNT(*) AS CancelledBeforeShipment
FROM
    Orders o
LEFT JOIN
    Shipments s ON o.OrderID = s.OrderID
WHERE
    o.OrderStatus = 'Cancelled'
    AND (s.ShipmentDate IS NULL OR o.CancelDate < s.ShipmentDate);
```

"To find how many orders were cancelled **before shipment**, I first joined the Orders table with the Shipments table using OrderID.

I focused only on rows where the OrderStatus was 'Cancelled', and then applied two conditions:
1. Either there's **no shipment date** (order never shipped), or
2. The **cancellation happened before the shipment date**.

This logic helps the business understand how many cancellations are due to user behavior or issues **before logistics were triggered**.

In the output, I counted **2 such orders**. That kind of insight can help reduce warehousing costs or improve customer satisfaction by enabling quicker cancellation handling.

If I had more fields like cancellation reason or payment method, I could segment further and give even richer insights.

2.66 Count the number of customers who have made a second purchase.

```
SELECT
    COUNT(*) AS CustomersWithSecondPurchase
FROM (
    SELECT
        CustomerID
    FROM
        Orders
    GROUP BY
        CustomerID
    HAVING
        COUNT(OrderID) >= 2
) AS RepeatCustomers;
```

To figure out how many customers have made a **second purchase**, I grouped the data by CustomerID and counted how many orders each one made.

Then, I filtered for customers who have made **2 or more orders** using the HAVING COUNT(OrderID) >= 2 clause.

The final outer query simply counted how many customers met that condition — in this example, it's **2 customers**.

This is super useful for evaluating **customer retention** or running **loyalty programs**. You could also enhance this by:
- Tracking when the second purchase occurred
- Comparing time between purchases
- Segmenting by product or channel

It's a basic but powerful metric in e-commerce.

2.67 Count the number of customers who have made a second purchase.

```
WITH BonusRanked AS (
    SELECT
        b.EmployeeID,
        e.Name,
        e.Department,
        b.BonusAmount,
        RANK() OVER (ORDER BY b.BonusAmount DESC) AS BonusRank
    FROM
```

```
        Bonuses b
    JOIN
        Employees e ON b.EmployeeID = e.EmployeeID
)
SELECT
    EmployeeID,
    Name,
    Department,
    BonusAmount
FROM
    BonusRanked
WHERE
    BonusRank = 1;
```

To identify the employees who received the **highest bonuses**, I first joined the Employees and Bonuses tables using EmployeeID.
I then used a **window function** — specifically, RANK() — to assign a ranking to each employee based on their BonusAmount, ordered in **descending order**.
This way, any tie for the highest bonus (like Charlie and Diana here) still gets the same rank.
Finally, I filtered to only keep those with BonusRank = 1, which means they received the **highest bonus value**.
This query gives visibility into top performers or high-reward team members and can help HR or finance teams identify **bonus distribution trends**.

2.68 Retrieve all transactions made during promotional periods.

```
SELECT
    t.TransactionID,
    t.CustomerID,
    t.TransactionDate,
    t.Amount,
    p.PromoName
FROM
    Transactions t
JOIN
    Promotions p
ON
    t.TransactionDate BETWEEN p.StartDate AND p.EndDate;
```

To identify which transactions occurred during **promotional periods**, I joined the Transactions table with the Promotions table based on whether the TransactionDate **falls between** the promotion's StartDate and EndDate.
I used a BETWEEN clause in the JOIN condition to map transactions to their corresponding promotions.
This lets us tag transactions with the promotion that might have influenced them. For instance, Transaction T002 happened during the 'Winter Bonanza' promo, and T005 during the 'Holiday Special'.
This kind of insight is incredibly useful for **measuring campaign effectiveness**, calculating **promo-attributed revenue**, and even understanding **seasonal shopping behavior**.
If we had additional columns like PromoType or Channel, we could slice it even further to make marketing decisions smarter.

2.69 Find the most common customer complaint category.

```
SELECT
    ComplaintCategory,
    COUNT(*) AS ComplaintCount
FROM
    CustomerComplaints
GROUP BY
    ComplaintCategory
ORDER BY
    ComplaintCount DESC
LIMIT 1;
```

To find the most common type of customer complaint, I queried the CustomerComplaints table and **grouped** the data by ComplaintCategory.

I used COUNT(*) to get how many complaints were made in each category and then **ordered the result in descending order** of count.

Using LIMIT 1, I fetched only the top result — in this case, the category **'Late Delivery'** with 3 complaints. This gives us direct visibility into what aspect of our service is causing the most customer dissatisfaction. Insights like this are vital for **prioritizing process improvements**, for example, tightening up the delivery chain or partnering with better logistics providers.

It could also be extended by tracking complaints over time or per region to uncover deeper trends.

2.70 Retrieve employees who have completed the most training programs.

```
WITH TrainingCounts AS (
    SELECT
        et.EmployeeID,
        COUNT(*) AS TrainingCompleted
    FROM
        EmployeeTraining et
    GROUP BY
        et.EmployeeID
)
SELECT
    e.EmployeeID,
    e.Name,
    e.Department,
    tc.TrainingCompleted
FROM
    TrainingCounts tc
JOIN
    Employees e ON tc.EmployeeID = e.EmployeeID
WHERE
    tc.TrainingCompleted = (
        SELECT MAX(TrainingCompleted)
        FROM TrainingCounts
    );
```

To identify which employees completed the **most training programs**, I started by creating a CTE (TrainingCounts) that groups training records by EmployeeID and counts how many training sessions each employee completed.

Then, I joined this result with the Employees table to retrieve employee names and departments.

Finally, I filtered the results to only show those employees whose training count equals the **maximum** across the dataset — using a subquery.

This ensures we account for **ties** if multiple employees completed the same highest number.

In our dataset, Alice from the Sales department completed **3 training programs**, more than anyone else.

This kind of analysis is often useful for **L&D (Learning and Development)** teams or **HR analytics**, especially when evaluating employee engagement or readiness for promotion or leadership roles.

Solutions to Advanced (71-101) Level Questions

2.71 Retrieve employees who have completed the most training programs.

```
WITH ProductSales AS (
    SELECT
        s.ProductID,
        p.ProductName,
        SUM(s.Quantity) AS TotalQuantity
    FROM
        Sales s
    JOIN
        Products p ON s.ProductID = p.ProductID
    GROUP BY
        s.ProductID, p.ProductName
),
RankedProducts AS (
    SELECT
        *,
        RANK() OVER (ORDER BY TotalQuantity DESC) AS SalesRank
    FROM
        ProductSales
)
SELECT * FROM RankedProducts;
```

To rank products based on sales volume, I first built a summary table that joins Sales with Products, and aggregates Quantity sold per product using SUM().
This gave me the total units sold per product.
Next, I used a window function — RANK() — to assign a rank to each product ordered by TotalQuantity DESC.
I used RANK() over DENSE_RANK() here because I wanted to allow for gaps in the ranks if there are ties (but I could switch depending on the business case).
The result clearly shows that the Bluetooth Speaker was the top-selling item with 25 units, followed by Water Bottles and Wireless Mice.
This insight can help stakeholders understand product performance, inform inventory decisions, or guide promotions.

2.72 Find customers who made multiple purchases in the same month.

```
SELECT
    c.CustomerID,
    c.CustomerName,
    DATE_TRUNC('month', o.OrderDate) AS OrderMonth,
    COUNT(*) AS OrdersInMonth
FROM
    Orders o
JOIN
    Customers c ON o.CustomerID = c.CustomerID
```

```
GROUP BY
    c.CustomerID, c.CustomerName, DATE_TRUNC('month', o.OrderDate)
HAVING
    COUNT(*) > 1;
```

■ If you're using MySQL, replace DATE_TRUNC('month', o.OrderDate) with DATE_FORMAT(o.OrderDate, '%Y-%m')

This analysis was designed to identify customers who placed more than one order in a single calendar month — useful for understanding repeat buying behavior.
First, I grouped orders by CustomerID and the month of their order (DATE_TRUNC was used to extract just the month part from the date).
I then counted the number of orders per customer per month, and filtered using HAVING COUNT(*) > 1 to find those with multiple purchases in the same month.
In our dataset, Alice and Bob both placed two orders each in June 2024 — making them valuable for potential loyalty programs or upselling strategies.
This type of insight can help drive customer segmentation or targeted retention campaigns.

2.73 Calculate the moving average of daily sales.

```
SELECT
    SaleDate,
    SUM(Amount) AS DailySales,
    ROUND(AVG(SUM(Amount)) OVER (
        ORDER BY SaleDate
        ROWS BETWEEN 2 PRECEDING AND CURRENT ROW
    ), 2) AS MovingAvg_3Day
FROM
    Sales
GROUP BY
    SaleDate
ORDER BY
    SaleDate;
```

■ This version assumes 1 row per sale per day. If multiple rows per day exist, we SUM() per date first and then compute the moving average.

To smooth out daily sales data and identify trends, I calculated a 3-day moving average using SQL's window function capability.
First, I aggregated daily totals using SUM(Amount) grouped by SaleDate.
Then, I applied a window function AVG(...) OVER (ROWS BETWEEN 2 PRECEDING AND CURRENT ROW) to look at each day and the two days before it — essentially creating a rolling window.
This technique helps detect short-term patterns like spikes or drops without being too reactive to single-day outliers.
For instance, while raw daily sales fluctuate, the moving average line reveals a gradual upward trend from June 1 to June 6.
This can be very useful in inventory planning, trend forecasting, or measuring promotion effectiveness over time.

2.74 Retrieve the top 3 customers with the highest lifetime value.

```
SELECT
    c.CustomerID,
    c.CustomerName,
    SUM(o.Amount) AS LifetimeValue
FROM
    Customers c
JOIN
    Orders o ON c.CustomerID = o.CustomerID
GROUP BY
    c.CustomerID, c.CustomerName
ORDER BY
    LifetimeValue DESC
LIMIT 3;
```

■ If your SQL flavor supports window functions and you prefer ranking:

```
WITH CustomerLTV AS (
    SELECT
        c.CustomerID,
        c.CustomerName,
        SUM(o.Amount) AS LifetimeValue,
        RANK() OVER (ORDER BY SUM(o.Amount) DESC) AS rank
    FROM Customers c
    JOIN Orders o ON c.CustomerID = o.CustomerID
    GROUP BY c.CustomerID, c.CustomerName
)
SELECT * FROM CustomerLTV WHERE rank <= 3;
```

I was asked to identify the **top 3 customers by lifetime value**, which is a great metric to understand who our **most valuable customers** are.
First, I joined the Customers and Orders tables on CustomerID. Then, I used SUM(Amount) to calculate **lifetime value**, grouping by customer.
Finally, I sorted the results in descending order of LifetimeValue and limited the output to 3 rows using LIMIT.
This helped surface that **Bob** was our highest-value customer with ₹700 in total purchases — a great candidate for loyalty rewards or high-touch service.
This kind of insight is critical for retention, segmentation, and personalized marketing.

2.75 Find the most frequent customer journey path on an e-commerce site.

```
WITH ordered_events AS (
    SELECT
        CustomerID,
        PageName,
        EventTime,
        ROW_NUMBER() OVER (PARTITION BY CustomerID ORDER BY EventTime) AS rn
    FROM Customer_Journey
```

```
),
paths AS (
    SELECT
        a.CustomerID,
        a.PageName || ' > ' || b.PageName || ' > ' || c.PageName AS journey_path
    FROM ordered_events a
    JOIN ordered_events b ON a.CustomerID = b.CustomerID AND a.rn + 1 = b.rn
    JOIN ordered_events c ON a.CustomerID = c.CustomerID AND a.rn + 2 = c.rn
)
SELECT
    journey_path,
    COUNT(*) AS frequency
FROM paths
GROUP BY journey_path
ORDER BY frequency DESC
LIMIT 1;
```

To understand how customers move through our e-commerce site, I analyzed the **customer journey paths** using the Customer_Journey table, which logs user interactions page by page.
First, I assigned a row number to each page view using ROW_NUMBER() over each CustomerID partitioned by event time. Then, I used self-joins to stitch together **3-page sequences** (like Homepage → ProductPage → Cart).
After building all possible 3-step journeys, I counted the frequency of each path to identify the most common one.
It turned out the most frequent journey was **'Homepage → ProductPage → Cart'**, which indicates customers are highly engaged with browsing and shortlisting — but we might want to check how many of them actually proceed to checkout or drop off here.
These insights can help us improve UX flow or run targeted remarketing campaigns.

2.76 Identify anomalies in transaction data.

We'll use the **IQR method** (Interquartile Range) to detect amount-based anomalies.

```
WITH stats AS (
    SELECT
        PERCENTILE_CONT(0.25) WITHIN GROUP (ORDER BY Amount) AS Q1,
        PERCENTILE_CONT(0.75) WITHIN GROUP (ORDER BY Amount) AS Q3
    FROM Transactions
),
anomalies AS (
    SELECT
        t.*,
        s.Q1,
        s.Q3,
        (s.Q3 - s.Q1) AS IQR
    FROM Transactions t
    CROSS JOIN stats s
)
SELECT
```

```
    TransactionID,
    CustomerID,
    Amount,
    TransactionDate
FROM anomalies
WHERE Amount < Q1 - 1.5 * IQR OR Amount > Q3 + 1.5 * IQR;
```

To identify anomalies in transaction data, I used a statistical approach based on the **Interquartile Range (IQR)**.
I started by calculating Q1 (25th percentile) and Q3 (75th percentile) of the Amount column using PERCENTILE_CONT. Then I computed the IQR = Q3 - Q1.
Any transaction amount that was below **Q1 - 1.5 * IQR** or above **Q3 + 1.5 * IQR** was flagged as an anomaly.
This method revealed one major outlier: a transaction of ₹980, which was well outside the typical range of ₹100–₹120.
Depending on the business context, this could signal fraud, pricing errors, or a need to investigate large-amount purchases for approval workflows.

2.77 Retrieve all customers who have downgraded their subscription.

```
WITH level_map AS (
    SELECT 'Premium' AS SubscriptionLevel, 3 AS level UNION
    SELECT 'Standard', 2 UNION
    SELECT 'Basic', 1
),
ranked_subs AS (
    SELECT
        s.CustomerID,
        s.SubscriptionLevel,
        lm.level,
        s.ChangeDate,
        ROW_NUMBER() OVER (PARTITION BY s.CustomerID ORDER BY s.ChangeDate) AS rn
    FROM Subscription_History s
    JOIN level_map lm ON s.SubscriptionLevel = lm.SubscriptionLevel
),
subs_with_prev AS (
    SELECT
        curr.CustomerID,
        curr.SubscriptionLevel AS CurrentLevel,
        prev.SubscriptionLevel AS PreviousLevel,
        curr.ChangeDate,
        curr.level AS current_rank,
        prev.level AS prev_rank
    FROM ranked_subs curr
    JOIN ranked_subs prev
      ON curr.CustomerID = prev.CustomerID AND curr.rn = prev.rn + 1
)
SELECT
```

```
    CustomerID,
    PreviousLevel,
    CurrentLevel,
    ChangeDate
FROM subs_with_prev
WHERE current_rank < prev_rank;
```

To identify customers who downgraded their subscriptions, I analyzed the Subscription_History table, which logs every change a customer makes over time. I first mapped each subscription level to a numeric rank — for example, Premium = 3, Standard = 2, Basic = 1 — to make comparison easy.
Then, using window functions, I assigned a row number to each subscription change per customer, ordered by date. I joined each current record with its previous one to compare subscription levels.
Any transition where the new rank was **lower** than the previous rank was flagged as a **downgrade**. The result highlighted customers like C001 and C003, who went from Premium to Basic or Standard to Basic respectively.
These insights can help the business take proactive steps, such as re-engagement campaigns, churn prevention strategies, or UX surveys.

2.78 Find the impact of discounts on total revenue.

```
SELECT
    SUM(Quantity * UnitPrice) AS Gross_Revenue,
    SUM(Quantity * UnitPrice * (1 - Discount)) AS Net_Revenue,
    SUM(Quantity * UnitPrice) - SUM(Quantity * UnitPrice * (1 - Discount)) AS
Discount_Impact,
    ROUND(100.0 *
        (SUM(Quantity * UnitPrice) - SUM(Quantity * UnitPrice * (1 - Discount)))
        / NULLIF(SUM(Quantity * UnitPrice), 0), 2
    ) AS Discount_Impact_Percentage
FROM Orders;
```

To measure the impact of discounts on total revenue, I calculated both **gross revenue** (pre-discount) and **net revenue** (after discount). I used the formula:
Net = Quantity × UnitPrice × (1 - Discount)
This gave me a true picture of what the business actually earned.
By subtracting net from gross revenue, I quantified the **total discount value** offered — in this case, ₹880.
I also computed the **percentage impact** by comparing the discount amount against gross revenue. We saw that discounts reduced our total revenue by around **13.33%**, which might be acceptable or alarming depending on business strategy.
This type of analysis is key when evaluating promotions or pricing changes — it helps in understanding whether discounts are converting into higher volume or just eating into profits.

2.79 Retrieve users who have the longest average session time.

```
SELECT
    UserID,
    ROUND(AVG(EXTRACT(EPOCH FROM (SessionEnd - SessionStart)) / 60), 2) AS
Avg_Session_Minutes
FROM UserSessions
```

```
GROUP BY UserID
ORDER BY Avg_Session_Minutes DESC;
```

To find users with the longest average session time, I calculated the **duration of each session** using the difference between SessionEnd and SessionStart. I converted that into minutes using EXTRACT(EPOCH FROM ...) / 60 for easier interpretation.

Then I grouped the data by UserID and used AVG() to find the **average session duration** for each user. Finally, I sorted the results in descending order so the users with the highest engagement appear at the top.

This kind of analysis is useful in user engagement studies — for example, in identifying your **most active or loyal users**, or detecting user behavior patterns that can guide product improvements or retention strategies.

2.80 Find the most common reason for order returns.

```
WITH ReturnStats AS (
    SELECT
        p.Category,
        r.ReturnReason,
        COUNT(*) AS ReturnCount
    FROM Returns r
    JOIN Orders o ON r.OrderID = o.OrderID
    JOIN Products p ON o.ProductID = p.ProductID
    GROUP BY p.Category, r.ReturnReason
),
TopReasonPerCategory AS (
    SELECT
        Category,
        ReturnReason,
        ReturnCount,
        RANK() OVER (PARTITION BY Category ORDER BY ReturnCount DESC) AS rk
    FROM ReturnStats
),
TotalOrders AS (
    SELECT
        p.Category,
        COUNT(*) AS TotalOrderCount
    FROM Orders o
    JOIN Products p ON o.ProductID = p.ProductID
    GROUP BY p.Category
),
TotalReturns AS (
    SELECT
        p.Category,
        COUNT(*) AS TotalReturnCount
    FROM Returns r
    JOIN Orders o ON r.OrderID = o.OrderID
    JOIN Products p ON o.ProductID = p.ProductID
```

```
    GROUP BY p.Category
)

SELECT
    t.Category,
    t.ReturnReason AS Most_Common_Return_Reason,
    t.ReturnCount,
    o.TotalOrderCount,
    r.TotalReturnCount,
    ROUND((r.TotalReturnCount::decimal / o.TotalOrderCount) * 100, 2) AS
ReturnRatePercent,
    CASE
        WHEN (r.TotalReturnCount::decimal / o.TotalOrderCount) > 0.10 THEN 'High
Return Rate'
        ELSE 'Normal'
    END AS ReturnRiskFlag
FROM TopReasonPerCategory t
JOIN TotalOrders o ON t.Category = o.Category
JOIN TotalReturns r ON t.Category = r.Category
WHERE t.rk = 1
ORDER BY ReturnRatePercent DESC;
```

This query helps surface **category-level return pain points**, prioritize efforts, and spot high-risk areas. It uses **window functions**, **CTEs**, and **conditional logic** to do a multi-dimensional analysis.
This would be a valuable report for **supply chain, product managers, and customer success teams** to improve the return experience and reduce revenue leakage.

2.81 Retrieve employees with the highest retention rate in each department.

```
WITH EmployeeTenure AS (
    SELECT
        e.EmpID,
        e.Name,
        d.DepartmentName,
        e.HireDate,
        COALESCE(e.ExitDate, CURRENT_DATE) AS EndDate,
        ROUND(DATE_PART('day', COALESCE(e.ExitDate, CURRENT_DATE) - e.HireDate) /
365.25, 2) AS TenureYears
    FROM Employees e
    JOIN Departments d ON e.DepartmentID = d.DepartmentID
),
RankedTenure AS (
    SELECT *,
        RANK() OVER (PARTITION BY DepartmentName ORDER BY TenureYears DESC) AS
DeptRank,
        CASE
            WHEN TenureYears >= 5 THEN 'Yes'
```

```
            ELSE 'No'
        END AS LongTenureFlag
    FROM EmployeeTenure
)

SELECT
    EmpID,
    Name,
    DepartmentName,
    HireDate,
    EndDate,
    TenureYears,
    DeptRank,
    LongTenureFlag
FROM RankedTenure
WHERE DeptRank = 1
ORDER BY DepartmentName;
```

To identify the most retained employees per department, I first calculated the tenure for each employee, using COALESCE to account for those still with the company.
Then I ranked them within their department using a RANK() window function.
Finally, I flagged those who have been with us for 5+ years, as they often indicate high loyalty, leadership potential, or cultural alignment.
This query can help HR teams focus retention programs or highlight employees suitable for promotions.

2.82 Find sales reps who exceeded their targets by the highest percentage.

```
WITH MonthlySales AS (
    SELECT
        SalesRepID,
        TO_CHAR(SaleDate, 'YYYY-MM') AS SaleMonth,
        SUM(Amount) AS TotalSales
    FROM Sales
    GROUP BY SalesRepID, TO_CHAR(SaleDate, 'YYYY-MM')
),
SalesPerformance AS (
    SELECT
        ms.SalesRepID,
        sr.RepName,
        ms.SaleMonth,
        ms.TotalSales,
        st.MonthlyTarget,
        ROUND(((ms.TotalSales - st.MonthlyTarget) * 100.0) / st.MonthlyTarget, 2)
AS PercentOverTarget,
        CASE
            WHEN ((ms.TotalSales - st.MonthlyTarget) * 1.0 / st.MonthlyTarget) >
0.5 THEN 'Yes'
```

```
            ELSE 'No'
        END AS ExceededBy50Percent
    FROM MonthlySales ms
    JOIN SalesTargets st
        ON ms.SalesRepID = st.SalesRepID AND ms.SaleMonth = st.Month
    JOIN SalesReps sr
        ON ms.SalesRepID = sr.SalesRepID
),
RankedPerformance AS (
    SELECT *,
            RANK() OVER (ORDER BY PercentOverTarget DESC) AS PerformanceRank
    FROM SalesPerformance
)

SELECT *
FROM RankedPerformance;
```

To identify top-performing sales reps, I started by aggregating monthly sales using TO_CHAR(SaleDate, 'YYYY-MM') for grouping. Then, I joined that data with the monthly targets to calculate how much each rep exceeded their target by — in percentage terms.

I used a CASE statement to flag reps who beat their target by more than 50%, which could help sales managers recognize exceptional over-performers.

Finally, I used a RANK() window function to order the reps by their performance. This structure helps not only in performance reviews but also in planning incentives or identifying training needs.

In a real-world BI tool, this could be visualized as a leaderboard with conditional coloring for high outliers.

2.83 Identify trends in customer churn.

```
WITH ChurnedCustomers AS (
    SELECT
        s.CustomerID,
        c.PlanType,
        DATE_TRUNC('month', s.StatusDate) AS ChurnMonth
    FROM SubscriptionStatus s
    JOIN Customers c ON s.CustomerID = c.CustomerID
    WHERE s.Status = 'Churned'
),
AllCustomersByMonth AS (
    SELECT
        DATE_TRUNC('month', s.StatusDate) AS StatusMonth,
        c.PlanType,
        COUNT(DISTINCT s.CustomerID) AS TotalCustomers
    FROM SubscriptionStatus s
    JOIN Customers c ON s.CustomerID = c.CustomerID
    GROUP BY DATE_TRUNC('month', s.StatusDate), c.PlanType
),
ChurnStats AS (
    SELECT
```

```
            a.StatusMonth,
            a.PlanType,
            COALESCE(c.ChurnCount, 0) AS ChurnedCustomers,
            a.TotalCustomers,
            ROUND((COALESCE(c.ChurnCount, 0) * 100.0) / a.TotalCustomers, 2) AS
ChurnRate
        FROM AllCustomersByMonth a
        LEFT JOIN (
            SELECT
                ChurnMonth,
                PlanType,
                COUNT(DISTINCT CustomerID) AS ChurnCount
            FROM ChurnedCustomers
            GROUP BY ChurnMonth, PlanType
        ) c
        ON a.StatusMonth = c.ChurnMonth AND a.PlanType = c.PlanType
)
SELECT *
FROM ChurnStats
ORDER BY StatusMonth, PlanType;
```

To analyze churn trends, I started by identifying customers who had a Churned status and grouped them by the month of churn and their subscription plan.

Then, I built a monthly snapshot of total active customers using SubscriptionStatus, grouped by month and plan type. Joining the churned data back with the active customer counts allowed me to compute monthly churn rates using simple division.

This analysis helps identify high-churn months (e.g., April for Basic users) and whether a specific **PlanType** is more prone to churn — potentially revealing issues in pricing, feature satisfaction, or competition.

This insight is great for churn prevention strategy — like targeted retention offers for Basic users or follow-ups after certain onboarding timeframes.

2.84 Retrieve transactions where the order amount deviates significantly from the average.

```
WITH Stats AS (
    SELECT
        AVG(OrderAmount) AS avg_order,
        STDDEV(OrderAmount) AS std_order
    FROM Transactions
),
FlaggedTransactions AS (
    SELECT
        t.*,
        s.avg_order,
        s.std_order,
        ABS(t.OrderAmount - s.avg_order) AS deviation
    FROM Transactions t
```

```
    CROSS JOIN Stats s
)
SELECT
    TransactionID,
    CustomerID,
    OrderDate,
    OrderAmount,
    avg_order,
    std_order,
    deviation
FROM FlaggedTransactions
WHERE ABS(OrderAmount - avg_order) > 2 * std_order;
```

To detect anomalous transactions, I first calculated the **average order amount** and **standard deviation** of all transactions using a CTE. This allowed me to set a statistical boundary — any transaction deviating by **more than two standard deviations** from the mean is likely to be an outlier.

In our case, one transaction stood out — with an amount of 500, which is well above the average of ~212 and over two standard deviations away. This could indicate a **data entry issue**, **fraudulent behavior**, or simply a **high-value order** that warrants investigation.

This technique can be generalized across customer segments, product types, or time windows to proactively monitor financial anomalies and strengthen operational integrity.

2.85 Find the most common time of day for purchases.

```
WITH TimeSlots AS (
    SELECT
        TransactionID,
        CustomerID,
        OrderDateTime,
        OrderAmount,
        CASE
            WHEN EXTRACT(HOUR FROM OrderDateTime) BETWEEN 5 AND 11 THEN 'Morning'
            WHEN EXTRACT(HOUR FROM OrderDateTime) BETWEEN 12 AND 16 THEN
'Afternoon'   WHEN EXTRACT(HOUR FROM OrderDateTime) BETWEEN 17 AND 20 THEN 'Evening'
            ELSE 'Night'
        END AS TimeOfDay
    FROM Transactions
),
TimeFrequency AS (
    SELECT
        TimeOfDay,
        COUNT(*) AS PurchaseCount
    FROM TimeSlots
    GROUP BY TimeOfDay
),
Ranked AS (
    SELECT *,
```

```
            RANK() OVER (ORDER BY PurchaseCount DESC) AS Rank
        FROM TimeFrequency
)
SELECT *
FROM Ranked
WHERE Rank = 1;
```

To identify when customers are most active, I created a custom time slot breakdown using a CASE statement:
Morning (5-11), Afternoon (12-16), Evening (17-20), Night (21-4).
I then grouped transactions by these slots to count how many purchases occurred in each window.
To identify the **most popular time(s)**, I applied a RANK() window function on the frequency count. In this dataset, both **Morning and Afternoon tied** as the most frequent time slots for purchases.
This analysis helps businesses understand **customer behavior trends** and can be used to **schedule push notifications**, **optimize inventory**, or **launch time-based promotions** for higher conversion.

2.86 Retrieve the percentage of customers who upgraded their plans.

```
WITH RankedPlans AS (
    SELECT
        CustomerID,
        PlanTier,
        ChangeDate,
        RANK() OVER (PARTITION BY CustomerID ORDER BY ChangeDate ASC) AS PlanOrder
    FROM CustomerPlans
),
FirstLastPlans AS (
    SELECT
        CustomerID,
        MAX(CASE WHEN PlanOrder = 1 THEN PlanTier END) AS FirstTier,
        MAX(CASE WHEN PlanOrder = 2 THEN PlanTier END) AS SecondTier
    FROM RankedPlans
    GROUP BY CustomerID
),
UpgradeFlags AS (
    SELECT
        CustomerID,
        FirstTier,
        SecondTier,
        CASE
            WHEN SecondTier > FirstTier THEN 1
            ELSE 0
        END AS Upgraded
    FROM FirstLastPlans
    WHERE FirstTier IS NOT NULL AND SecondTier IS NOT NULL
)
SELECT
    ROUND(100.0 * SUM(Upgraded) / COUNT(*), 2) AS PercentageUpgraded
```

```
FROM UpgradeFlags;
```

To calculate the percentage of customers who upgraded their plans, I first ranked their plan history by date using RANK() within each customer group.
Then I isolated the first and second plans for each customer—this allows us to compare their plan progression.
 Using a simple CASE statement, I flagged those customers who moved to a higher plan tier (e.g., from Tier 1 to Tier 2 or Tier 3).
Finally, I calculated the upgrade rate by dividing the count of upgraded customers by the total number of customers with multiple plan records.
In our sample, two out of three customers upgraded, giving us an upgrade percentage of **66.67%**.
This kind of analysis is important to evaluate **customer satisfaction**, **product stickiness**, and can inform **targeted upsell strategies**.

2.87 Find the correlation between product ratings and return rates.

```
WITH ProductRating AS (
    SELECT
        ProductID,
        ROUND(AVG(Rating), 2) AS AvgRating
    FROM ProductReviews
    GROUP BY ProductID
),
ProductReturns AS (
    SELECT
        ProductID,
        COUNT(*) AS TotalOrders,
        SUM(IsReturned) AS TotalReturns,
        ROUND(1.0 * SUM(IsReturned) / COUNT(*), 2) AS ReturnRate
    FROM OrderDetails
    GROUP BY ProductID
),
ProductStats AS (
    SELECT
        r.ProductID,
        p.AvgRating,
        r.ReturnRate
    FROM ProductReturns r
    JOIN ProductRating p ON r.ProductID = p.ProductID
)
SELECT
    CORR(AvgRating, ReturnRate) AS RatingReturnCorrelation
FROM ProductStats;
```

To explore the relationship between how well customers rate products and how often those products are returned, I approached it by joining two datasets — one for reviews and another for order returns.
First, I calculated the **average product rating** using a GROUP BY on the ProductReviews table.
Separately, I calculated each product's **return rate** as the number of returns divided by total orders in the OrderDetails table.

After combining both results, I used the **CORR()** function to compute the **Pearson correlation coefficient** between the two numeric columns: AvgRating and ReturnRate.
In our sample data, we found a correlation of **-0.87**, indicating a **strong inverse relationship** — meaning products with **lower ratings tend to be returned more**. This can inform both our **product quality teams** and **customer satisfaction efforts**.

2.88 Retrieve employees who have been promoted more than once.

```
SELECT
    EmployeeID,
    COUNT(*) AS PromotionCount
FROM
    EmployeePromotions
GROUP BY
    EmployeeID
HAVING
    COUNT(*) > 1;
```

Deep Dive (Advanced Context):
If you want to go one step further, you could also return promotion trajectory by concatenating all previous & new titles, or calculating average time between promotions:

```
-- (Optional) Show promotion path
SELECT
    EmployeeID,
    STRING_AGG(CONCAT(PreviousTitle, ' → ', NewTitle), ' | ' ORDER BY
PromotionDate) AS PromotionPath,
    COUNT(*) AS PromotionCount
FROM
    EmployeePromotions
GROUP BY
    EmployeeID
HAVING
    COUNT(*) > 1;
```

Output (Optional Advanced View):

EmployeeID	PromotionPath	PromotionCount
E101	Junior Analyst → Analyst | Analyst → Senior Analyst | Senior Analyst → Lead Analyst	3

2.89 Find regions where average order value is higher than the global average.

```
WITH MonthlyRegionAvg AS (
    SELECT
        DATE_TRUNC('month', OrderDate) AS OrderMonth,
        Region,
        AVG(OrderAmount) AS RegionalAvg
```

```
    FROM Orders
    GROUP BY DATE_TRUNC('month', OrderDate), Region
),
MonthlyGlobalAvg AS (
    SELECT
        DATE_TRUNC('month', OrderDate) AS OrderMonth,
        AVG(OrderAmount) AS GlobalAvg
    FROM Orders
    GROUP BY DATE_TRUNC('month', OrderDate)
),xx
Comparison AS (
    SELECT
        r.OrderMonth,
        r.Region,
        r.RegionalAvg,
        g.GlobalAvg,
        CASE
            WHEN r.RegionalAvg > g.GlobalAvg THEN 1 ELSE 0
        END AS Outperforming
    FROM MonthlyRegionAvg r
    JOIN MonthlyGlobalAvg g ON r.OrderMonth = g.OrderMonth
),
ConsecutiveOutperformance AS (
    SELECT *,
        ROW_NUMBER() OVER (PARTITION BY Region ORDER BY OrderMonth) -
        ROW_NUMBER() OVER (PARTITION BY Region, Outperforming ORDER BY
OrderMonth) AS grp
    FROM Comparison
),
RankedPerformance AS (
    SELECT Region, COUNT(*) AS consecutive_months
    FROM ConsecutiveOutperformance
    WHERE Outperforming = 1
    GROUP BY Region, grp
    HAVING COUNT(*) >= 3
)
SELECT DISTINCT Region, consecutive_months
FROM RankedPerformance;
```

To solve this, I first extracted the **month-wise average order value globally**, and then calculated the **region-wise average order value per month**.
I used a **window function (ROW_NUMBER or COUNT)** to track **how many consecutive months** a region has outperformed the global average.
Using a **Common Table Expression (CTE)** structure made the logic more modular and readable.
This kind of analysis is crucial in **long-term strategic planning**, especially when tracking **consistent high-performance regions** rather than one-off spikes.

2.90 Retrieve customers who have interacted with customer service more than 5 times.

```
WITH FilteredInteractions AS (
    SELECT
        CustomerID,
        InteractionType,
        COUNT(*) AS InteractionCount
    FROM CustomerServiceLogs
    WHERE InteractionDate >= CURRENT_DATE - INTERVAL '6 months'
    GROUP BY CustomerID, InteractionType
),
SummedInteractions AS (
    SELECT
        CustomerID,
        SUM(InteractionCount) AS TotalInteractions
    FROM FilteredInteractions
    GROUP BY CustomerID
)
SELECT
    f.CustomerID,
    f.InteractionType,
    f.InteractionCount,
    s.TotalInteractions
FROM FilteredInteractions f
JOIN SummedInteractions s
  ON f.CustomerID = s.CustomerID
WHERE s.TotalInteractions > 5
ORDER BY s.TotalInteractions DESC;
```

In real-world analytics, it's not just about raw counts — it's about identifying patterns. So for this problem, I filtered interactions to the last 6 months and grouped by customer and interaction type.
I then aggregated to count how many interactions occurred per customer and filtered to highlight only those with more than 5 interactions. This helps the business segment customers who might be at risk of churn or need priority support.
I used **date filtering**, **grouping**, and **conditional aggregation** to build a scalable solution for customer experience teams.

Real-World Application:
This query can be plugged into a **churn prediction model** or used by **customer success teams** to prioritize outreach. You could further expand it by:
- Joining with a customer satisfaction score table
- Creating a dashboard to track high-frequency interaction customers
- Building alerts using triggers or scheduled reports

2.91 Identify the impact of marketing campaigns on sales volume.

```
WITH CampaignWindow AS (
```

```
SELECT
    c.CampaignID,
    c.CampaignName,
    c.StartDate,
    c.EndDate,
    DATEADD(day, -7, c.StartDate) AS PreStartDate,
    DATEADD(day, 7, c.EndDate) AS PostEndDate
  FROM Campaigns c
),
SalesWithPeriods AS (
  SELECT
    cw.CampaignID,
    cw.CampaignName,
    s.SaleDate,
    s.Amount,
    CASE
      WHEN s.SaleDate BETWEEN cw.PreStartDate AND DATEADD(day, -1, cw.StartDate)
THEN 'Pre-Campaign'
      WHEN s.SaleDate BETWEEN cw.StartDate AND cw.EndDate THEN 'During-Campaign'
      WHEN s.SaleDate BETWEEN DATEADD(day, 1, cw.EndDate) AND cw.PostEndDate THEN
'Post-Campaign'
      ELSE NULL
    END AS SalePeriod
  FROM Sales s
  JOIN CampaignWindow cw
    ON s.SaleDate BETWEEN cw.PreStartDate AND cw.PostEndDate
)
SELECT
  CampaignID,
  CampaignName,
  SalePeriod,
  COUNT(*) AS TotalSales,
  ROUND(SUM(Amount)::numeric, 2) AS TotalRevenue,
  ROUND(AVG(Amount)::numeric, 2) AS AvgDailySale
FROM SalesWithPeriods
WHERE SalePeriod IS NOT NULL
GROUP BY CampaignID, CampaignName, SalePeriod
ORDER BY CampaignID,
        CASE
          WHEN SalePeriod = 'Pre-Campaign' THEN 1
          WHEN SalePeriod = 'During-Campaign' THEN 2
          WHEN SalePeriod = 'Post-Campaign' THEN 3
        END;
```

To measure campaign effectiveness, I segmented the sales timeline into three periods for each campaign: Pre-campaign, During-campaign, and Post-campaign windows.
I calculated the **average daily sales** in each phase, per campaign, using a date-based join between campaigns and sales.

This approach allows the business to directly compare the impact of marketing activities and spot which campaigns actually drove sales lifts — instead of assuming correlation.

Real-World Business Use:
- **Marketing Team Insight**: Spot which campaigns actually lift sales vs. flat ones.
- **Budget Optimization**: Redirect resources to campaigns with proven "During" impact.
- **Data Storytelling**: Feed this into dashboards for C-suite or investor presentations.

2.92 Retrieve the top 10% of customers by spending.

```
WITH CustomerSpending AS (
  SELECT
    o.CustomerID,
    c.CustomerName,
    SUM(o.OrderAmount) AS TotalSpent
  FROM Orders o
  JOIN Customers c ON o.CustomerID = c.CustomerID
  GROUP BY o.CustomerID, c.CustomerName
),
RankedCustomers AS (
  SELECT *,
        NTILE(10) OVER (ORDER BY TotalSpent DESC) AS SpendingDecile
  FROM CustomerSpending
)
SELECT CustomerID, CustomerName, TotalSpent
FROM RankedCustomers
WHERE SpendingDecile = 1   -- Top 10%
ORDER BY TotalSpent DESC;
```

To identify high-value customers, I calculated total spending per customer and used a **window function** to rank them.
Then, I determined the **10th percentile rank** using the total customer count and selected those customers whose ranks fell within the **top 10%**.
This approach helps the business in identifying top spenders for loyalty programs, personalized marketing, and retention strategies.

Business Impact:
- **Customer segmentation**: Identify and target top-tier customers.
- **Retention strategy**: Offer loyalty rewards to top 10% customers.
- **Predictive modeling**: Use these insights to create customer lifetime value (CLV) segments.

2.93 Find trends in seasonal product sales.

```
SELECT
    EXTRACT(YEAR FROM s.sale_date) AS year,
    CONCAT('Q', EXTRACT(QUARTER FROM s.sale_date)) AS quarter,
    p.category,
    SUM(s.quantity) AS total_units_sold,
    SUM(s.total_amount) AS total_revenue
```

```
FROM
    sales s
JOIN
    products p ON s.product_id = p.product_id
GROUP BY
    year, quarter, p.category
ORDER BY
    year, quarter, total_units_sold DESC;
```

To analyze seasonal trends in product sales, I joined the sales and products tables to understand what categories were being sold and when. I then extracted the **quarter** and **year** from the sale_date and aggregated total quantities and revenue per category per quarter. This gave insights into which categories are popular in different seasons. For instance, if 'Winter Wear' peaks in Q1 and Q4 consistently, that's a strong seasonal trend."

How You'd Conclude Your Answer in the Interview:
"This analysis clearly shows seasonal patterns—for example, 'Winter Wear' performs best in Q1 and Q4, aligning with colder months, while 'Summer Care' and 'Summer Wear' products like Sunscreen and T-shirts peak in Q2 and Q3. Such insights can help in inventory planning, targeted marketing, and pricing strategies. If this were a real-world scenario, I'd take it further by adding weather data or regional sales variation."

2.94 Identify customers who have abandoned carts frequently.

```
SELECT
    c.customer_id,
    c.name,
    c.email,
    COUNT(*) AS abandoned_cart_count
FROM
    cart ct
JOIN
    customers c ON ct.customer_id = c.customer_id
WHERE
    ct.purchased_flag = FALSE
    AND ct.added_date >= CURRENT_DATE - INTERVAL '6 months'
GROUP BY
    c.customer_id, c.name, c.email
HAVING
    COUNT(*) >= 2
ORDER BY
    abandoned_cart_count DESC;
```

To identify frequent cart abandoners, I focused on customers who added products to their cart but never purchased them. I filtered out any cart entries where the purchased_flag was FALSE. Then I grouped by customer_id and counted the number of such abandoned carts. Finally, I filtered to only show customers with more than 2 abandoned carts in the last 6 months. This approach helps the business pinpoint which users are regularly dropping off before checkout, indicating UX issues or pricing barriers.

2.95 Retrieve orders where the actual delivery time was significantly delayed.

```
SELECT
    o.order_id,
    c.name AS customer_name,
    p.product_name,
    o.order_date,
    o.expected_delivery_date,
    d.actual_delivery_date,
    DATE_PART('day', d.actual_delivery_date - o.expected_delivery_date) AS
delay_days
FROM
    orders o
JOIN
    deliveries d ON o.order_id = d.order_id
JOIN
    customers c ON o.customer_id = c.customer_id
JOIN
    products p ON o.product_id = p.product_id
WHERE
    d.actual_delivery_date > o.expected_delivery_date + INTERVAL '3 days'
ORDER BY
    delay_days DESC;
```

In this analysis, I focused on detecting delivery inefficiencies. I joined the orders and deliveries tables to compare the actual_delivery_date with the expected_delivery_date. Then, I calculated the delay in days. To filter only the significantly delayed orders, I set a threshold of more than 3 days. I included customer and product info to provide context for which customers and products were most affected. This type of insight is critical for operations and customer experience teams.

2.96 Find the impact of social media engagement on customer purchases.

```
WITH engagement_scores AS (
    SELECT
        customer_id,
        platform,
        SUM(likes + comments * 2 + shares * 3) AS total_engagement_score
    FROM
        social_media_engagement
    GROUP BY
        customer_id, platform
),
customer_orders AS (
    SELECT
        o.customer_id,
        COUNT(DISTINCT o.order_id) AS order_count,
        SUM(o.total_amount) AS total_spent
```

```
    FROM
        orders o
    GROUP BY
        o.customer_id
)
SELECT
    e.customer_id,
    c.name,
    e.platform,
    e.total_engagement_score,
    co.order_count,
    co.total_spent
FROM
    engagement_scores e
JOIN
    customers c ON e.customer_id = c.customer_id
LEFT JOIN
    customer_orders co ON e.customer_id = co.customer_id
ORDER BY
    e.total_engagement_score DESC;
```

To assess how social media engagement influences purchases, I created an **engagement score** (likes + comments × 2 + shares × 3) for each interaction. Then I joined this with the orders and sessions data to track if customers who engaged on social platforms actually placed an order. I also analyzed which **platforms** had the highest conversion and revenue. This gives us actionable insight on which social media channels are driving meaningful customer activity.

2.97 Retrieve all orders where the shipping address was modified post-purchase.

```
SELECT
    o.order_id,
    c.name AS customer_name,
    p.product_name,
    o.order_date,
    sac.old_address,
    sac.new_address,
    sac.change_date,
    DATE_PART('day', sac.change_date - o.order_date) AS days_after_order
FROM
    orders o
JOIN
    shipping_address_changes sac ON o.order_id = sac.order_id
JOIN
    customers c ON o.customer_id = c.customer_id
JOIN
    products p ON o.product_id = p.product_id
WHERE
```

```
    sac.change_date > o.order_date
ORDER BY
    days_after_order DESC;
```

In this task, I focused on identifying all orders where a shipping address was changed **after** the order was placed, which could point to fraud risk, operational delay, or customer indecision. I joined the orders and shipping_address_changes tables on order_id, filtered where change_date > order_date, and calculated how many days after the order the address was updated. I also included customer details to help the operations or fraud team follow up if needed.

2.98 Retrieve all orders where the shipping address was modified post-purchase.

```
WITH suspicious_quick_signup_txn AS (
    SELECT
        t.txn_id,
        c.customer_id,
        'High amount shortly after signup' AS reason
    FROM
        transactions t
    JOIN customers c ON t.customer_id = c.customer_id
    WHERE
        t.status = 'Success'
        AND t.amount > 800
        AND t.txn_date <= c.signup_date + INTERVAL '1 day'
),
suspicious_failed_then_success AS (
    SELECT
        t.txn_id,
        t.customer_id,
        'Multiple failed txns before success' AS reason
    FROM
        transactions t
    WHERE
        t.status = 'Success'
        AND EXISTS (
            SELECT 1 FROM transactions f
            WHERE
                f.customer_id = t.customer_id
                AND f.status = 'Failed'
                AND f.txn_date = t.txn_date
        )
),
suspicious_multiple_locations AS (
    SELECT
        t.txn_id,
        t.customer_id,
        'Multiple city orders same day' AS reason
```

```
    FROM
        transactions t
    JOIN devices d ON t.customer_id = d.customer_id
    WHERE
        t.txn_date = d.login_time
    GROUP BY t.txn_id, t.customer_id
    HAVING COUNT(DISTINCT d.location) > 1
)
SELECT
    DISTINCT t.customer_id,
    c.name,
    s.txn_id,
    t.amount,
    t.txn_date,
    s.reason
FROM
    (
        SELECT * FROM suspicious_quick_signup_txn
        UNION
        SELECT * FROM suspicious_failed_then_success
        UNION
        SELECT * FROM suspicious_multiple_locations
    ) s
JOIN transactions t ON t.txn_id = s.txn_id
JOIN customers c ON c.customer_id = s.customer_id
ORDER BY t.txn_date;
```

To flag potential fraudulent patterns, I first defined some logical criteria. These included:
- High-value transactions made **within 1 day of signup** (possible fake accounts).
- Multiple **failed transactions** followed by a success (could be brute-force attempts).
- Orders made from **two different cities within the same day** by the same user (might indicate identity compromise).

By layering these signals, we can prioritize cases for manual review or algorithmic scoring. I joined transactions, customers, and supporting logs, and filtered based on these red flags.

2.99 Find the correlation between product reviews and sales performance.

```
WITH avg_ratings AS (
    SELECT
        product_id,
        ROUND(AVG(rating), 2) AS avg_rating,
        COUNT(*) AS total_reviews
    FROM product_reviews
    GROUP BY product_id
),
sales_summary AS (
    SELECT
```

```
        product_id,
        SUM(quantity) AS total_units_sold,
        ROUND(SUM(quantity * price), 2) AS total_revenue
    FROM order_items
    GROUP BY product_id
)
SELECT
    p.product_id,
    p.product_name,
    p.category,
    COALESCE(a.avg_rating, 0) AS avg_rating,
    COALESCE(a.total_reviews, 0) AS total_reviews,
    COALESCE(s.total_units_sold, 0) AS total_units_sold,
    COALESCE(s.total_revenue, 0) AS total_revenue
FROM
    products p
LEFT JOIN avg_ratings a ON p.product_id = a.product_id
LEFT JOIN sales_summary s ON p.product_id = s.product_id
ORDER BY avg_rating DESC;
```

To understand whether better product reviews drive sales, I calculated the **average rating** for each product and joined it with **sales volume** data. I aggregated review ratings from product_reviews and total quantities sold from order_items, grouping by product_id.
Then I matched these metrics to the products table to provide context. This allows us to **visually or statistically explore** correlation, e.g., by exporting this for plotting or regression in Python.
This insight is useful for **product strategy, marketing prioritization, and customer satisfaction tracking**.

2.100 Retrieve the average number of items per order per month.

```
WITH order_item_counts AS (
    SELECT
        oi.order_id,
        EXTRACT(MONTH FROM o.order_date) AS order_month,
        SUM(oi.quantity) AS total_items
    FROM order_items oi
    JOIN orders o ON oi.order_id = o.order_id
    GROUP BY oi.order_id, EXTRACT(MONTH FROM o.order_date)
),
monthly_summary AS (
    SELECT
        order_month,
        COUNT(order_id) AS total_orders,
        SUM(total_items) AS total_items_in_month,
        ROUND(AVG(total_items), 2) AS avg_items_per_order
    FROM order_item_counts
    GROUP BY order_month
```

```
)
SELECT
    order_month,
    total_orders,
    total_items_in_month,
    avg_items_per_order
FROM monthly_summary
ORDER BY order_month;
```

To understand order behavior over time, I calculated the **total number of items per order**, then grouped this by **month** to find the **average number of items per order each month**.

This is valuable for inventory planning and customer behavior analysis. If we see a spike in average items in a certain month, we might correlate it with promotions, seasonality, or campaigns. I used EXTRACT(MONTH FROM order_date) to group orders and took the **sum of item quantities** for each order from the order_items table.

2.101 Identify the most profitable customer segment.

```
WITH customer_segments AS (
    SELECT
        customer_id,
        gender,
        city,
        CASE
            WHEN age BETWEEN 18 AND 24 THEN '18-24'
            WHEN age BETWEEN 25 AND 34 THEN '25-34'
            WHEN age BETWEEN 35 AND 44 THEN '35-44'
            ELSE '45+'
        END AS age_group
    FROM customers
),
segment_revenue AS (
    SELECT
        cs.gender,
        cs.city,
        cs.age_group,
        SUM(o.total_amount) AS total_revenue
    FROM orders o
    JOIN customer_segments cs ON o.customer_id = cs.customer_id
    GROUP BY cs.gender, cs.city, cs.age_group
)
SELECT
    gender,
    city,
    age_group,
    total_revenue
```

```
FROM segment_revenue
ORDER BY total_revenue DESC
LIMIT 5;
```

To find the most profitable customer segment, I joined orders with customers and created **age groups** dynamically using CASE statements. I then aggregated total order revenue per segment by combining **gender, city, and age group**.

This query gives decision-makers a clear picture of who their most valuable customers are. For example, if women aged 25–34 in Mumbai consistently generate high sales, marketing can double down on this segment. This is a great use case for **targeted advertising, regional strategy, and churn prevention**.

Final Thoughts

Thank you for joining me on this hands-on journey through data analysis using real-world datasets. Whether you're a beginner exploring data analytics with Python, or a working professional brushing up on SQL for data insights, this book was designed to give you both theoretical understanding and practical application.

With the help of real business scenarios, you've worked through challenges involving data cleaning, visualization, query building, and interpreting key metrics. These skills are foundational in any data analyst or business intelligence role.

As data continues to shape every industry — from eCommerce to healthcare — I hope you'll revisit these examples as a reference guide in your career or learning path.